PRESENTED BY

Alex Kaufman

WESTMINSTER SCHOOLS

SMYTHE
GAMBRELL
LIBRARY

1996
Thomas Grantham

BAR MITZVAH

A Jewish Boy's Coming of Age

by Eric A. Kimmel
Illustrated by Erika Weihs

VIKING

VIKING
Published by the Penguin Group
Penguin Books USA Inc., 375 Hudson Street, New York, New York 10014, U.S.A.
Penguin Books Ltd, 27 Wrights Lane, London W8 5TZ, England
Penguin Books Australia Ltd, Ringwood, Victoria, Australia
Penguin Books Canada Ltd, 10 Alcorn Avenue, Toronto, Ontario, Canada M4V 3B2
Penguin Books (N.Z.) Ltd, 182-190 Wairau Road, Auckland 10, New Zealand

Penguin Books Ltd, Registered Offices: Harmondsworth, Middlesex, England

First published in 1995 by Viking, a division of Penguin Books USA Inc.

1   3   5   7   9   10   8   6   4   2

Text copyright © Eric A. Kimmel, 1995
Illustrations copyright © Erika Weihs, 1995
All rights reserved

LIBRARY OF CONGRESS CATALOGING-IN-PUBLICATION DATA
Kimmel, Eric A.
Bar Mitzvah: a Jewish boy's coming of age / Eric A. Kimmel; illustrated by Erika Weihs. p.   cm.
ISBN 0-670-85540-5
1. Bar mitzvah—Juvenile literature. 2. Bar mitzvah—Anecdotes—Juvenile literature.
[1. Bar mitzvah. 2. Judaism.] I. Weihs, Erika. II. Title.
BM707.K56 1995 — 296.4'424—dc20 94-34956 CIP AC

Printed in U.S.A.
Set in Granjon

For my father,
who would have liked this book.
E.A.K.

Special thanks for their contributions to the jacket montage to Aryeh Benjamin; Benny Benjamin; Moshe Benjamin; J. Levine Books and Judaica, New York City; Meiersdorf Photography, Jerusalem; Sharon Strassfeld; and Betsy Platkin Teutsch. And especially to Stephanie Garcia for her creative energy and flair in putting everything together.

I want to thank my editor, Deborah Brodie, for her vision and persistence in persuading an initially reluctant author that writing a book about the meaning of the bar mitzvah ceremony was a good idea. I would also like to acknowledge the help of those scholars who generously shared their insight and expertise with us during the preparation of this book, especially Yocheved Herschlag Muffs, Judaica consultant, and Professor David G. Roskies of the Jewish Theological Seminary of America.

E. A. K.

CONTENTS

....

BAR MITZVAH

A Jewish Boy's Coming of Age

INTRODUCTION

Rabbi Avraham Yaakov of Sadagora once told his followers, "We learn not only from the natural world, but from modern inventions, too."

"What can you learn from a railroad train?" one of his followers asked.

"Only one second late, but you still lose everything," the rabbi replied.

"What can you learn from the telegraph?" another asked him.

"Every word is counted, and you pay for each one."

"And the telephone?"

"What is said here is heard there."

This story is a good way to begin a book about becoming bar mitzvah. Just as the Sadagora rabbi, who lived in Bukovina in the nineteenth century, drew spiritual truths from modern devices, so do old and new ideas blend together to create the Jewish celebration called bar mitzvah.

The bar mitzvah ceremony is an ancient one that has become extremely important in contemporary Jewish life. It is so important that, seventy years ago, a parallel celebration called the bat mitzvah was created for girls. Before that time, the bar mitzvah experience was exclusively for boys. The creation of the bat mitzvah is only one example of how new ideas and understandings have reshaped the age-old tradition. In the course of this book, we will find many more.

As important as bar and bat mitzvah ceremonies are considered today, it is surprising to learn that Judaism has no official rules about either. The Torah and Talmud, the main sources of Jewish tradition, say nothing about them. No one is required to have a bar or bat mitzvah. A person who goes through the ceremony is not more Jewish than one who does not. Yet the experience of becoming bar or bat mitzvah is regarded as such an important life-cycle event that many Jewish men and women who did not participate in a bar or bat mitzvah ceremony as adolescents will voluntarily spend hours preparing for one as adults.

What makes this experience so important to modern Jews?

This book was written to explain what it means for a Jewish boy to become bar mitzvah. A companion volume, by Barbara Diamond Goldin, will focus on the bat mitzvah experience for girls. My aim is to explain what a bar mitzvah is, how the ceremony developed, and its significance for Jews today. In some ways, trying to understand the bar mitzvah experience is like playing a multi-level video game: As soon as you master one challenge, you find yourself facing another. To understand what happens during the bar mitzvah ceremony, you need to understand the Torah ritual and how it fits into the pattern of Jewish worship. To understand that, you need to know something about Judaism, what it shares with Christianity and Islam, the two other great Western religions, and how it differs from them.

The first chapters of this book present some basic understandings about religion and culture. These are followed by a brief history of Judaism and its main texts, the Torah and the Talmud. Finally, we come to the Sabbath synagogue service and the bar mitzvah ceremony itself, as it was celebrated in the past and as it is celebrated today. Several prominent scholars have reviewed the text to make sure that it gives an accurate picture of contemporary and traditional Jewish religious practice.

Throughout the book, I have tried to give a sense of the richness of contemporary Jewish life. My descriptions of synagogue procedure are based on traditional Eastern European practice, since the majority of American Jews are of Ashkenazic ancestry. However, I do not mean to imply that this is the only acceptable way. The patterns of modern Jewish worship are as varied as the colors in Joseph's coat, and we are all the richer for it.

There is far more to celebrating a bar mitzvah than most people realize. The ceremony encompasses every aspect of Jewish culture, which one could study for a lifetime without coming to the end.

Rabbi Tarfon, a second-century sage, once remarked, "You are not required to complete the task, yet you are not free to withdraw from it." There is also a Jewish proverb that says, "All journeys begin with difficulty—the first step."

Let us take that step together.

E.A.K.

INTERVIEW ···

I loved my bar mitzvah. It was the most important thing I'd ever done. For the first time, I really felt proud to be Jewish. You see, where I live in Eugene, Oregon, Jews are a definite minority. And when you're a minority, you have to put up with a lot of slurs, stereotypes, and basic ignorance. There were plenty of times when I wanted to be like everybody else. But when I celebrated my bar mitzvah, I felt as if I really accomplished something important, and everybody in my life who mattered knew it was important and came to celebrate with me. It was such a powerful feeling that I was sorry when it was over. I wanted to do it again. In one sense I did, because I learned to chant another haftarah, a reading from the Prophets, which I just did in our synagogue last week.

Something else happened to me on my bar mitzvah that changed my life. I received a book called The Words of Dr. Martin Luther King, Jr. *I don't know who gave it to me. It was one of those mysterious gifts that just appear. I became fascinated by what I read. I wanted to know more, so I went on to read everything I could find by Dr. King. Then I went on to read*

4

the writings of Malcolm X, Marcus Garvey, and others. Since then I've become heavily involved in political activities, fighting "isms"—anti-Semitism, racism, sexism, and homophobia. This has made me feel even more Jewish, and has spurred me to continue my Hebrew education, because you need knowledge to fight the hate and the lies that are all around us.

Seth Rubinstein
Bar Mitzvah, 1991

LUCKY THIRTEEN

How different cultures help boys become men

TODAY I AM A HUMAN BEING

Be strong as a panther, light as an eagle, swift as a gazelle, and bold as a lion to carry out the will of your Father in heaven.

Rabbi Yehudah ben Tema
The Sayings of the Fathers, *second century* C.E.

When a Jewish boy is thirteen years and one day old, he celebrates becoming bar mitzvah. It seems unusual to celebrate a major life experience at this age, since many people regard thirteen as an ill-omened number. Friday the thirteenth is the unluckiest day in the calendar. Ancient Greek farmers avoided sowing crops on the thirteenth day of the month. The number thirteen has strong associations with black magic and witchcraft. Thirteen was the devil's number. There were twelve witches in a coven, and the devil made thirteen. A "baker's dozen," twelve plus one, was originally called the "devil's dozen."

However, in Jewish tradition, there is nothing unlucky or evil about the number thirteen. On the contrary, thirteen has positive associations. God is seen as having thirteen attributes. And thirteen is the age of becoming bar mitzvah, when, according to the Jewish religion, boys take on the responsibilities of adulthood.

Coming of Age

Thirteen is an important age in Jewish tradition. But it is also a significant time in other cultures as well. American society regards the teenage years as a distinct period of life. A teenager is no longer a child, yet still not an adult. American teenagers have their own styles, music, language, and customs. Some would even consider teenagers to be a distinct subculture.

There is an important reason that this particular period of life is so significant. For most boys, the years from about twelve to fourteen mark the onset of puberty. Important biological changes take place as children become adolescents. Over the next few years, a boy will get taller and stronger. His voice will deepen. He will develop facial and body hair. He may look like an adult, and will frequently act in a mature, responsible manner. Yet at other times he will feel and act very much like a child.

For fifteen hundred years, Jewish law has considered thirteen to be the age of male majority, when a boy assumes responsibility for his own actions. (For girls, the age of majority is twelve.) In the words of *The Sayings of the Fathers,* a second-century text, "Thirteen is for fulfilling commandments." If a twelve-year-old boy stole a handful of candy from a store, his parents were held responsible. Even if they knew nothing about the theft and were nowhere near the store at the time, they still had to pay for the damage. It was their responsibility to teach their son to distinguish right from wrong and to supervise his conduct until they were certain he knew the difference.

Similarly, if a twelve-year-old boy violated a religious law, such as desecrating the Sabbath or failing to say the proper blessing before eating, the guilt for the sin fell on his parents. As a minor, a twelve-year-old could not be expected to fully understand the consequences of his actions and could not be held responsible for them.

This changed the moment a boy reached the age of thirteen years and one day, the legal age of majority. A thirteen-year-old was considered old enough to know the difference between right and wrong and to act accordingly. He had to answer for his own sins; he could no longer blame them on his parents. A special blessing which many parents say on the occasion of their son's becoming bar mitzvah states this fact in no uncertain terms: "Blessed are You, Lord, Our God, Ruler of the Universe, Who has relieved me of responsibility for this boy."

These are never easy words for a parent to say, especially when a boy may not be mature enough to assume the responsibilites of adulthood. There is a story about Rabbi Yekhiel Mikhal of Zoltchov in Galicia, who was worried about his youngest son, Ze'ev Wolf. The boy was lazy, irresponsible, and disobedient. As the day of his son's bar mitzvah celebration approached, the rabbi ordered a pair of tefillin, prayer boxes, from the town scribe. The scribe brought the leather boxes and the parchments inscribed with the biblical verses to Rabbi Yekhiel Mikhal. The rabbi held them in his hand for a long time. As he thought of his son, tears ran down his cheeks and fell into the open boxes. Then he returned them to the scribe and told him to seal them. On the day that Ze'ev Wolf put the tefillin on for the first time, his personality changed completely. He became kind and loving, diligent in his studies, and helpful to all. In time he became a famous rabbi like his father. The moral of this story? Some parents may feel that only a miracle can turn their child into a responsible adult. However, miracles do happen.

Privileges and Responsibilities

Becoming thirteen in Jewish tradition is similar to becoming eighteen in the United States today. Eighteen-year-olds can vote, drive a car, join the military, and handle their own affairs without adult supervision. On the down side, eighteen-year-olds who commit crimes are tried and sentenced as adults. Society expects them to behave in a mature, responsible manner and requires that behavior from them.

Similarly in the Jewish world, adult privileges go with adult responsibilities. A thirteen-year-old becomes eligible to be counted as a member of a *minyan,* the quorum of ten Jews needed to hold a prayer service. He can be given an *aliyah,* the significant honor of being called up during the service to read from the Torah. A thirteen-year-old can testify as a witness in a Jewish court of law, a *bet din.* If qualified, he can even preside over the court as a judge.

As if to emphasize the idea of thirteen as a special age, medieval legend tells us that many important biblical figures began fulfilling their destinies when they reached the age of thirteen. Abraham rejected idol worship when he was thirteen years old. At thirteen, Jacob received the blessing of the firstborn from his father, Isaac. Jacob's son, Joseph, was sold into slavery in Egypt when he was thirteen. Thirteen-year-old David slew the Philistine giant, Goliath. Solomon, David's son, became king of Israel when he was thirteen years old.

Boys into Men

Thirteen can be an exciting age. Yet it can also be a difficult and confusing time, too. Robert Bly, a poet and philosopher who has written about men's issues, points out in his book *Iron John* that boys sometimes become involved in street gangs because they are trying to become men, but don't know how.

Boys trying to be men can be a dangerous, unstable, and easily manipulated group. Cultural and religious communities all over the world have recognized the need for young males to be fully integrated into their societies. Otherwise, they are likely to cause trouble for themselves and everyone else. For this reason, various groups have developed special ceremonies to help young men make the transition from childhood to adulthood. These ceremonies are called rites of passage. They celebrate and confirm an individual's passing from one stage of life to another. By ritualizing the biological and psychological changes that are taking place, society provides boys with instruction, support, role models, and a clearly marked path to follow. An Australian, Native American, or African rite of passage may appear vastly different from a bar mitzvah ceremony. Yet they all serve the same purpose. They show boys how to become men.

The Aborigines of Australia have a custom called the walkabout. As a boy grows up, he learns the skills of survival by watching and helping the older men of his group. He learns how to locate food and water, how to find his way in a trackless desert, how to make the tools and weapons he needs.

When he feels he has mastered these skills, the boy leaves his group and goes off by himself to an isolated area—walking about—for six months to a year. He might not encounter another human being during this entire time. A walkabout is a hard test. There are no second chances. Accidents, mistakes, and bad luck claim many lives. However, if the boy has learned the lessons of survival, he will return to his group, confident in his own skills, prepared to take on a man's role, for he has passed the test of manhood.

In some traditional Native American cultures, when a boy felt that he was ready to take on a man's role, he would go on a vision quest. He came alone to a "place of power." This was a place where people felt close to the spirits. It might be on a mountaintop or on a bluff overlooking a river. It might be in a cave or beside a spring. Here the boy began his fast. He would eat no food and drink no water until his vision appeared. Throwing off his clothes, he endured the hot sun by day and the cold wind at night, all the while praying to the spirits to grant him a vision. If the vision was late in coming, he might slash his arms and body with his knife, or even cut off a fingertip to show the spirits how well he could endure

12

pain. If the spirits found him worthy, they would send him a vision. A supernatural being would appear to the boy in the shape of an animal. It might take on the form of a bear, a bison, an eagle, a coyote. This spirit would teach the boy how to live in harmony with the supernatural and the natural worlds. The spirit would be the boy's guardian and source of power for as long as he lived.

In some traditional African cultures, the rite of passage includes all boys in a village who arrive at the age of puberty at the same time. On a certain day, the men of the village suddenly disappear. A short time later, a group of fierce strangers (the boys' fathers and uncles in disguise) descends on the village. The terrified boys run to their mothers, but their mothers cannot protect them. The strangers drag them away to the forest.

For the next several days or weeks, the boys undergo a spiritual boot camp. They are smeared with mud and ashes. They are given little food. They are not allowed to sleep more than a few hours at a time. The boys must prove their physical and spiritual strength by enduring discomfort without complaint and by submitting to insults and humiliation without protest. At the same time, their captors begin instructing the boys in what it means to be a man. They relate stories about the great men of their nation. They talk about the tests the boys will face and tell them how to behave when the time comes.

The last test is the most important. Each boy must prove his ability to endure pain as his body is marked with the signs of manhood. In some groups, one of the older men knocks out each boy's two front teeth with a stone. In others the men slash the boy's arms, legs, face, and body with a series of cuts to form a distinctive pattern of

scars. Boys are usually circumcised at this time. Each boy must endure all this pain in silence. He must not cry out or struggle. To do so would mean disgrace and failure.

For the final part of the ceremony, the boys are made to crawl between an older man's legs. This symbolizes their second birth as men. When the boys return home, their mothers and sisters pretend not to know them. They are completely different from the children they once were. They are boys no longer. Now they are men.

The Jewish Path to Manhood

A boy preparing himself to become bar mitzvah is getting ready to assume a man's role according to the ancient traditions of the Jewish people. He must concentrate and study to acquire the skills and knowledge he needs. He must learn about Judaism, its history and beliefs. He must study Hebrew, the ancient language of the Jewish people, which unites Jews all over the world. He must reflect and meditate on what being Jewish means today. A Jewish education is not acquired overnight. It requires sacrifice—although nothing as drastic as having your teeth knocked out—but it does demand time and effort. A boy preparing for a bar mitzvah ceremony may have to give up leisure time, sports, and other favorite activities.

Finally, the boy must come before his family, his friends, his neighbors, his congregation, and his community, and, through the bar mitzvah ceremony, show the world that he is no longer a child. By his own efforts, he will have earned the right to begin taking on the privileges and responsibilities of adulthood.

INTERVIEW ···

I killed a man on my bar mitzvah. He was the first one. There were plenty of others after him.

After the Nazis killed everybody in our Polish town, I escaped to the forest to join the partisans. We had a rabbi in our band. He kept track of the days so he would know when there was a Jewish holiday. Don't ask me how he did it. We didn't have a calendar. I think he followed the phases of the moon.

On this one day, he asked me when my birthday was. I told him. Then he said, "Next Shabbos will be your bar mitzvah." He announced it to the whole band. When the day came, they had a little party for me. They opened a bottle of vodka and everybody drank. That was the first time they let me drink vodka with them.

That night our commander invited me to go on a mission. It seems this peasant had been bringing food to a Jewish family hiding in the forest. He helped them as long as they had money, and when the money ran out, he turned them in to the Nazis for the reward. He thought nobody knew about it, but we had ways of finding out these things.

When we got to his house, we kicked in the door and pulled him out of bed. He started begging for his life. He swore he was innocent. He didn't know how the Nazis found out about the Jews in the forest. Then we knew he was guilty, because no one had said a word about them.

We tied his hands behind his back and dragged him outside. He fell on his knees and begged us to spare him. Our commander handed me his pistol.

"Here's your present, bar mitzvah boy. Do you think you can do it?"

I nodded. I was a little nervous, but I knew what to do. I pointed the pistol at the man's head and pulled the trigger. He pitched forward, dead. His blood splashed on my boots.

Everybody congratulated me afterwards. "Yashar koyach," they said. That's what everyone says after you read from the Torah. It means "May your strength increase," or something like that.

How did I feel about what I did? I felt proud. I felt fine. I gave that skunk what he deserved, and I hoped I'd have the chance to do it again.

That's how I became a man.

Abe Pomerantz
Bar Mitzvah, 1943

TORAH, TALMUD, AND TRADITION

The origins and teachings of Judaism

Working miracles is no great trick. Anyone who has reached a certain level of spiritual development can do it. But to be a Jew—now that's hard!

> The Yehudi of Przysucha
> Poland, eighteenth century

When a boy takes on the responsibilities of an adult member of the Jewish people, he becomes part of an ancient tradition going back almost four thousand years.

Judaism, Christianity, and Islam

Judaism is the oldest of the three major religions of the Western world. The other two, Christianity and Islam, derive many of their beliefs and practices from Judaism. This is no coincidence, for Jesus and Paul, the founders of Christianity, were Jews. Muhammad, the founder of Islam, had close ties to the Jewish tribes of Arabia and based many of the teachings of Islam on what he knew and admired about Judaism.

Judaism is an "ethical monotheistic" religion. *Ethics* refers to a system of moral values: the rules and principles of proper conduct. The word *monotheism* is derived from two Greek words meaning "one" and "god." Jews believe in one God who brought the world and the universe into being. This God is a God of justice and mercy who requires all human beings to treat each other with consideration and respect. God has always existed. God has no beginning and no end. In the words of *Adon Olam,* a famous hymn, "God was, and is, and shall ever be, in glory."

Christianity and Islam are also ethical monotheistic religions, but they differ from Judaism in important ways. Christians believe that one aspect of God, the Son, became a human being who lived and died as a man, Jesus of Nazareth. According to Christians, God is sympathetic to human hopes, fears, and sufferings because he experienced them himself. Christians also believe that Jesus is the Messiah, the Redeemer whose coming was foretold by the biblical prophets.

Christianity is an inspiring faith. However, no Jew can accept its teaching about Jesus and remain Jewish. The differences between Jewish and Christian belief can be illustrated by the following story.

A Roman emperor once said to Shimon ben Shetach, a famous rabbi, "Show me this god you worship."

Shimon ben Shetach led the emperor out to a field. He pointed to the sun and said, "Look at that."

"I cannot," the emperor said. "It dazzles my eyes."

Shimon ben Shetach told him, "You cannot look at the creation. How then can you possibly expect to behold the Creator?"

Similarly, a Jew would say to a Christian, "If a human being came within a million miles of the sun, that person would be vaporized. The sun is only a minor star. How can the force which creates and sustains a universe of galaxies—thousands upon thousands of suns—be contained in human flesh?"

Many Jews acknowledge Jesus as a teacher and important historical figure. However, no Jews accept him as the Messiah and they cannot accept him as divine.

By contrast, Islam's concept of the Oneness of Allah is closer to the understanding of God in Judaism. The word *Allah* is related to *El,* a Hebrew term for God. This is no accident, because Islam has more in common with Judaism than any other religion. One reason for this is that Islam's founder, the prophet Muhammad, based many of his religious ideas on what he knew and understood about Judaism. Another is that Arabs and Jews both speak Semitic languages and share some similar customs and cultural values. Arabic and Hebrew, the languages of the Koran and the Torah, are cousins, related to each other in roughly the same way as French is related to Spanish. Muslim and Jewish traditions teach that Arabs and Jews are descended from the same ancestor, Abraham. The great figures of the Bible also appear in the Koran—Abraham as Ibrahim, Moses as Musa, Aaron as Harun, David as Da'ud, and Solomon as Suleiman.

Islam is an inspiring faith for hundreds of millions of people all over the world. Many of its traditions and practices resemble those of Judaism. However, as with Christianity, there are important aspects of Islam that Jews cannot accept. Jews reject the idea that the teachings of the Torah have been replaced by a new prophet with a new message. Nor do they believe that there is One True Religion for all human beings. Jews look forward to a time when all people will worship God and treat one another with justice and compassion. They do not believe it is necessary for everyone to practice the Jewish religion.

Abraham, the First Jew

Christianity begins with Jesus. Islam begins with Muhammad. Judaism also traces its beginnings to a remarkable individual. His name was Abraham. According to tradition, he was born almost four thousand years ago in the Mesopotamian city of Ur, in what is now modern Iraq. Abraham is the spiritual founder of Judaism and the ancestor of the Jewish people. According to Jewish traditions, he was the first human being to recognize the Oneness of God.

The Book of Genesis tells us that God commanded Abraham to leave his birthplace and go to a land that God would show him. God promised to give this beautiful, fruitful land to Abraham and his descendants. In biblical times, this land was known as Canaan. Today, part of that land is the modern state of Israel. The emotional and religious ties with this land, nurtured and cherished by the Jewish people for centuries, go back to this ancient promise.

Abraham and his followers called themselves Hebrews—*Ivriim*. Some scholars suggest that the word means "from the other side," since Abraham came "from the other side" of the Euphrates River.

Later, the term *B'nai Yisrael*—"the Children of Israel" or Israelites—is used in the Bible. *Israel* is another name for Jacob, Abraham's grandson. The word *Jew* was not used until centuries later.

Jew is a derivation of the name Judah. Judah was Abraham's great-grandson. His descendants, and those of his brothers and nephews, became known as the Twelve Tribes of Israel. The tribe of Judah was the largest and most powerful of the tribes. It survived to become an independent kingdom and later a province of the Roman empire called Judea.

Abraham is the spiritual father of the Jewish people and Judah is its namesake, but the true founder of the Jewish religion is Moses. Moses must rank as one of the greatest religious figures of all time. His teachings gave rise to three major religions. Without Moses, Judaism, Christianity, and Islam would not exist.

Moses, the Lawgiver

Moses is an Egyptian name, similar to Thutmose and Amose, the names of several Egyptian rulers. According to the Book of Exodus, the Egyptians enslaved the Hebrews living in their country out of fear that they might rise up and join their enemies. When this failed to reduce the Hebrew population, Pharaoh, the king of Egypt, ordered all newborn male children put to death. Moses' mother, Yochebed, and his sister, Miriam, put the infant Moses in a floating cradle and set it adrift on the Nile. Pharaoh's daughter found it. At Miriam's suggestion, she hired Yochebed to be his nurse, not knowing she was his mother. Even though Moses was raised as an Egyptian prince, he still retained contact with his people.

A popular legend about Moses' childhood is not in the Bible. According to this story, the royal astrologers came before Pharaoh with a warning. The stars foretold that the foundling taken from the river would overthrow the power of Egypt. However, Pharaoh had grown fond of the boy and didn't want to kill him. He decided on a test. Two jars were placed before the infant Moses. One contained jewels; the other, hot coals. If the baby reached for the jewels, it meant that he might one day reach for Pharaoh's crown. But if he reached for the coals, there was nothing to fear.

As the Egyptians watched, the infant Moses, intrigued by the sparkling jewels, stretched out his hand toward them. But God sent an angel down from heaven. The angel pushed Moses' hand into the burning coals. When the baby brought his hand to his mouth to cool his fingers, a piece of hot coal burned his tongue. From then on, Moses spoke with a speech defect. In later years, whenever he came before Pharaoh or before the Children of Israel, his brother Aaron had to speak for him, because he himself was a poor speaker.

Moses grew up among the Egyptians, but he never forgot his people. One day he struck down and killed an overseer whom he saw beating a Hebrew slave. Afraid for his life, Moses fled from Egypt and lived for a time among the desert tribes of Midian. One day, while tending his sheep, Moses heard God speak to him out of a burning bush. God commanded Moses to return to Egypt to free his people.

Pharaoh refused to release the Israelites. As a result, ten terrible plagues struck the Egyptians, their crops, and cattle. The last plague was the most frightening of all. Every firstborn male in Egypt died in one night, including Pharaoh's own son. Only then did Pharaoh allow the Israelites to leave. However, he soon had second thoughts. Pharaoh led an army of chariots in pursuit of the fleeing Israelites. But God split the Red Sea and Moses led his people across. When the Egyptians followed, the sea closed and drowned them all.

Moses is the greatest leader and teacher the Jewish people ever had throughout their long history. Through Moses, God freed their ancestors from slavery in Egypt. Through Moses, God rescued them at the Red Sea. With God's help, Moses led them for forty years in the Sinai desert. Most important of all, God chose Moses to receive the Torah at Mount Sinai.

The Torah

This was an event of monumental importance. God entered into a covenant—a legal relationship—with the people of Israel. This covenant established an entirely new relationship with God, as well as a new way of life. One legend tells how God offered this covenant to all the nations of the earth. Only the people of Israel chose to accept it without question.

What was this covenant that Moses received on Mount Sinai? It is usually depicted as the tablets of the Ten Commandments, but the word *Torah,* meaning "law" or "teaching," implies much more than that. The Torah includes all the rules, obligations, history, poetry, and literature contained in the first five books of the Bible. These are known as the Pentateuch or the Five Books of Moses. The word *Torah* is also used to include all subsequent interpretations and adaptations of those rules to be made in the future.

This idea is important, because it establishes the principle that God gave people the right to use their intelligence to interpret the laws given to them.

A story from the time of the Romans illustrates this principle. A group of rabbis were arguing an issue of religious law. Rabbi Eliezer ben Hyrcanus offered an opinion. It was rejected. Rabbi Eliezer protested the decision. "I am right and I can prove it. If my opinion is correct, let the stream outside this study house flow backward."

The stream began to flow backward.

Rabbi Joshua ben Hananiah, who led the majority, said, "A stream doesn't prove anything."

Rabbi Eliezer continued, "If my opinion is correct, let the walls of the study house prove it."

The walls started leaning toward them.

Rabbi Joshua held firm, and told the walls to go back to their place.

Finally Rabbi Eliezer said, "Let Heaven itself bear witness that my opinion is the correct one."

A voice came from out of the sky. "Why do you reject Rabbi Eliezer's opinion? He is right in every case."

To which Rabbi Joshua responded, "The Torah is not in heaven. We pay no attention to voices."

This principle made the Torah a living document. It was not locked in stone. It was not the property of mystical fanatics. Reason and logic could be used to adapt its teachings to changing times and conditions. Perhaps the greatest miracle of Sinai is that a religious code given to a tribe of nomadic shepherds at the time when the pyramids were new continues to be a source of guidance even in the closing years of the twentieth century.

The idea of the continuing validity of the Torah and its teachings is another crucial difference between Judaism, Christianity, and Islam. Christians believe that the validity of the Torah, which they call the Old Covenant, ended with the coming of Jesus. Jesus' life and death brought about a different relationship, a New Covenant, between God and humanity. For this reason, Christians refer to the Jewish Bible as the Old Testament. The books relating the story of Jesus and his followers are called the New Testament. Similarly, Muslims believe that while both the Torah of the Jews and the New Testament of the Christians contain important teachings, the full truth of God's revelation was not given to humanity until Muhammad received the Koran from God through the angel Gabriel.

Jews believe that God gave the Torah to Moses in written form so that it could be read and studied by all. The rabbis considered the study of Torah a form of further revelation; they called it Oral Torah.

For this reason, Jews throughout the centuries have felt a religious devotion to literacy and education. Studying God's Torah was the obligation of every Jew. One could not be pious and illiterate. Study was as important as prayer.

The Oral Torah

The Torah is not easy to understand. One simple sentence can take on worlds of meaning. For example, the Torah says, "You shall not boil a baby goat in its mother's milk" (Deuteronomy, 14:21). What does that mean? The Torah doesn't say. This puzzling sentence has been interpreted to mean that meat and dairy products should not be served or eaten together. Furthermore, separate cookware, dishes, and eating utensils must be used for meat and dairy meals. This separation of meat and dairy products forms one important part of *kashrut,* which includes all the laws determining whether or not food is kosher and permissible to be eaten. Thus, a series of complex dietary laws developed from one obscure sentence in the Torah.

Over the centuries, rabbis and scholars have had to deal with many such issues. Like the prohibition against mixing milk and meat, some of the most important practices of Judaism are not specifically mentioned in the written Torah, but were derived from the Oral Torah, the memorized interpretations that went with it. The Oral Torah grew more complex with each generation. Yet little of it had ever been collected, organized, or even written down, in any systematic manner.

Recognizing the danger that important teachings might be lost because of the unsettled political conditions of the time, a generation of rabbis began the process of collecting, editing, and publishing the Oral Torah. Their work was completed by one of the greatest scholars in Jewish history, Rabbi Judah HaNasi (170–217 C.E.). His work is called the Mishnah. Divided into six main sections, the Mishnah categorizes the laws related to agriculture, commerce, religious observance, and other aspects of human interaction.

One of the best known sections of the Mishnah is the *Pirke Avot,* the sayings of the Fathers. This collection of the words of famous Rabbis emphasizes ethical and moral principles.

For example: *"The day is short, the work is plentiful, the workers are lazy, the wage is generous, and the Master is insistent."* Rabbi Tarfon

29

"Pray for the government. If people did not fear it, they would eat each other alive." Rabbi Chaninah

"Let your neighbor's honor be as precious to you as your own, and do not anger easily." Rabbi Eliezer

Compiling the Mishnah was an outstanding achievement. However, just as the Oral Torah grew around the written Torah, so too did a similar body of teachings begin to grow around the Mishnah. These interpretations, called Gemara, together with the Mishnah itself, form the body of Jewish teaching known as the Talmud.

Generations of Jews have devoted their lives to studying the Talmud. For centuries the Talmud, even more than the Torah itself, has been regarded as the cornerstone of the Jewish religion, for it deals with the vital question of how God's laws are to be applied to daily life. Religious law, civil law, ethics, morality, ritual observance—every conceivable form of human activity came under the scrutiny of the sages of the Talmud.

Modern Branches

The idea of the Torah, which includes the Mishnah and Talmud as well as the Five Books of Moses, remains an important component of Jewish life today. The main division between Jews in the United States—traditional vs. liberal—is based largely on how they view the Torah's ancient teachings. One word of caution: It is hard to generalize about Jewish groups. Judaism does not have a hierarchy or an official set of beliefs as does, for example, the Roman Catholic Church. Jewish congregations work out their own patterns of worship. There are many variations, even within the same broad group.

Orthodox Jews make the Torah's teachings the foundation of their lives. They believe that the Torah is as valid in the modern age as it was in the time of the Mishnah. Orthodox Jews study Torah and Talmud on a daily basis and continue to observe all the traditional rules governing everyday life and conduct. Yet Orthodox Jews have never denied the importance of modern technology. Many outstanding scientists and doctors are Orthodox; however, Orthodox Jews insist that science and technology be used in ways consistent with the teachings of the Torah.

Hasidic Jews are distinct sects within Orthodox Judaism. There are many Hasidic groups, ranging from the fairly liberal Lubavitch to the extremely conservative Satmar Hasidim. In general, Hasidic Jews are known for their distinctive dress and for the great intensity and joy with which they worship. The Hasidic movement began in eighteenth-century Poland with an inspired teacher known as the Baal Shem Tov (Master of the Good Name). Hasidim follow the teachings of certain charismatic rabbis, called rebbes, who are believed to have a special relationship with God.

Liberal Jews fall into three main groups, Reform, Conservative, and Reconstructionist. The distinctions among them have more to do with the details of traditional practice in their worship services and daily lives than in significant differences in their beliefs. Conservative Jews tend to be more traditional than Reform Jews, although here again it is a mistake to generalize. There are Reform Jews who observe the dietary laws of kashrut and Conservative Jews who do not.

An offshoot of the Conservative movement, Reconstructionism defines Jewishness as a distinct culture, an entire civilization, of which religion is only one, and not necessarily the most important, aspect.

Liberal Jews see the Torah as part of an ongoing dialogue between God and the Jewish people. History has a purpose and the Jewish people have a role to play in it. Through the Torah, God shows the Jewish people what that role is.

This role changes with time, as does the Oral Torah. The tribal customs of the early Israelites evolved into the teachings of the Talmud. Similarly, Liberal Jews believe the Torah for the modern age is necessarily different from the Torah of the past. Ritual practices such as *kashrut* are viewed as a matter of individual choice. On the other hand, Liberal Jews believe that a modern Torah requires each individual to join with others to bring about an end to violence, injustice, and bigotry. Reform Jews, in particular, have a strong tradition of working together with followers of other religions to further the cause of social justice and world peace.

Unity in Diversity

In addition to the main orthodox and liberal groups, there are also numerous informal Jewish fellowships called *havurot,* whose members develop their own traditions from sources as diverse as the Baal Shem Tov and Bob Dylan.

Finally, there are people who are not religious at all, but who still define themselves as Jewish. Some enjoy the holiday and family rituals. Some are attracted to Jewish history and literature. Others are committed to Jewish moral and ethical values. Many express their Jewishness in a political context, by fighting against anti-Semitism or by working through Zionist groups and organizations for the benefit of Israel and Jewish people all over the world. Some merely like Jewish food, while others enjoy being around Jews.

Just as there is no single definition of *American,* there is no one way of defining a *Jew.* Such diversity should be expected and even welcomed. This is because Judaism is more than a religion. It is a worldwide civilization with its own rich history, culture, language, and unique set of social and spiritual values that have changed, grown, and developed throughout the centuries, and will continue to do so for ages to come.

INTERVIEW ···

I think the worst part about becoming bar mitzvah is that it happens at the same time you're going through puberty. Your body is going through all these changes; your emotions are going up and down, and while all that's going on, you have to prepare for this major performance.

There was a terrible blizzard on the day of my bar mitzvah. The whole city was snowed in. And yet the synagogue was full. These people walked through seven-foot drifts to be there. The snow was so high my five-foot grandmother couldn't get up the steps. They had to carry her in. Those people could have stayed home. Nobody would have blamed them if they did. But they came to show their respect for my parents, and they wanted to be there for me.

The people in our synagogue followed the Torah and haftarah readings closely, and if you made a mistake, they'd all call out the correct word. I got through without making one error.

Then I read a little lecture I had written about the Torah portion. This is called a Dvar Torah. *That was the part of my bar mitzvah that I liked best. I enjoyed the challenge of coming up with something original. I hope to become a published writer some day. Looking back, I realize that my* Dvar Torah *was the first extended piece of original writing I'd ever done.*

Nathan Jacoby
Bar Mitzvah, 1983

A HOUSE OF PRAYER
AND STUDY

The synagogue and Jewish worship

Lord, I love the house You dwell in, and the place where Your

Glory abides.

Shaharit, *Morning Prayer Service*

A Jewish house of worship is called a synagogue. The word comes from *synagoge,* a Greek word meaning "assembly." Reform Jews also use the word *temple*. Other terms that are commonly used are *Bet Haknesset* (House of Assembly), *Bet Tefilah* (House of Prayer), and *Bet Midrash* (House of Study). The different names describe the different functions a synagogue building serves: community center, meeting hall, place of prayer, sanctuary, and place of study.

Synagogue Form and Function

Unlike mosques and churches, synagogues do not have distinctive exterior architectural features. One reason is that the Jewish religion has no rules governing what a synagogue must look like. In some places, Christian and Muslim authorities imposed limits on synagogues' size and decoration to emphasize the inferiority of Judaism. In some Muslim countries, for example, a synagogue cannot be taller than a mosque.

Synagogues were frequent targets for hostile mobs. Polish synagogues of the sixteenth century, such as the ones at Pinsk and Zholkva, were built as forts. They had thick masonry walls, narrow windows, and places on the roof where marksmen could shoot down at attackers. For the most part, synagogues built before the eighteenth century tended to be unobtrusive structures that blended in with the neighboring buildings.

Refuge and Sanctuary

Once inside the synagogue doors, Jews were in a different world. Here they found shelter from hostile surroundings. The synagogue was their special place, a second home, which they decorated with love and care. The interior of a synagogue might include polished brass and silver lamps, carved wooden chairs and benches, paneled walls, colorful carpets, and velvet curtains adorned with gold and silver embroidery. Although the biblical law prohibiting the making of graven images discouraged portraits of people and the type of representative art that could be found in a medieval cathedral, since the first century, the walls of synagogues were frequently painted with biblical texts, scenes from the Bible, and fanciful beasts and flowers.

The Torah Scroll

When Orthodox and Conservative Jews worship in a synagogue, they face east, in the direction of Jerusalem (except for worshipers in Asia, who face west to face Jerusalem). The ark containing the Torah scrolls occupies a prominent position against the eastern wall. Just as the Torah is the center of the Jewish religion, so the Torah scrolls are the heart of the synagogue.

A Torah is a handwritten parchment scroll containing the first five books of the Bible: Genesis, Exodus, Leviticus, Numbers, and Deuteronomy. A scroll is an ancient form of book; in Jewish eyes, it has an age-old majesty that no other form of book can equal.

It takes a professional scribe, or *sofer,* about a year to write a Torah. In addition to being an experienced calligrapher, a scribe must be a person of outstanding piety. The scribe must also be familiar with the complex rules that govern the making of a Torah.

A Torah must be written on specially prepared parchment taken from the skin of a kosher animal (an herbivore with split hooves, such as a cow, sheep, or goat). The words must be written in straight lines of a certain length, with a prescribed number of lines and columns to each sheet of parchment. Only specially prepared indelible ink can be used. The letters must be written with a quill pen that comes from a kosher bird (such as a goose or turkey) slaughtered in the approved manner.

To make sure no errors creep in, a scribe may not write the text from memory. He must copy the words from a guide for professional scribes.

A Torah looks extremely plain compared to other handwritten manuscripts. Since the accuracy of the text comes first, scribes are not permitted to add illustrations or any artistic flourishes other than those prescribed. The one exception to this rule occurred two thousand years ago in the Egyptian city of Alexandria. According to the Talmud, Alexandrine scribes were accustomed to apply a thin layer of gold leaf to the letters spelling out any of the words for God.

Although this custom is no longer observed, scribes still make special preparations before writing out any of God's names. A scribe begins his day by going to the *mikveh,* the ritual bath, to make sure he is in a state of purity. He will meditate, concentrating his thoughts and making sure he is in a properly devout state of mind before writing the holy letters. There are practical as well as religious reasons for taking such great care. Should a scribe make a mistake while writing out one of the names of God, it cannot be scratched out or erased. The scribe is required to discard the entire sheet of parchment rather than commit the sin of blotting out God's name. The parchment cannot be used for any other purpose, nor can it be thrown away. It must be stored in a special place with other damaged religious articles until it can be buried in a Jewish cemetery.

When a Torah is finished, the parchments are sewn together and the long scroll is attached to two wooden rods. The scroll is rolled tightly around these rods and tied with a sash or linen band.

• BAR MITZVAH •

Torah Ornaments

Sephardic communities, those whose cultural roots lie in Spain, North Africa, Central Asia, and the Middle East, keep the Torah in a hinged wooden box called a *tik*. The box is covered with silver, stamped leather, or velvet. Its top resembles the graceful domes of Middle Eastern buildings. The Torah is never removed from its box. The box opens to allow the scroll to be read. The rods of the scroll are decorated with elaborate silver ornaments. The rods protrude through the top of the box and are used to roll the scroll to the proper reading.

Ashkenazic communities, those whose cultural roots lie in Europe, cover the Torah with a velvet mantle. This mantle is beautifully embroidered with traditional symbols such as the lions of Judah, the menorah, and the Ten Commandments. Holes in the top of the mantle allow it to be pulled down over the rods. As in Sephardic congregations, these rods are decorated with elaborate silver ornaments. One type of ornament is in the shape of a crown, symbolizing the majesty of God and the Torah.

Ashkenazic communities also hang a silver breastplate over the front of the Torah. This calls to mind the breastplate that was worn by the high priest in the ancient Temple during biblical times. A silver pointer hangs beside the breastplate on a separate chain. The pointer is called a *yad* or "hand." This is an appropriate name, because the end of the *yad* resembles a hand with a pointing index finger.

The *baal korei*, the person reading from the Torah, uses the *yad* to point out the words of the text to make sure he doesn't lose his

40

place. He also uses it to indicate the starting and stopping places for the person saying the blessings. A *yad* is used for two reasons. One is to ensure an accurate reading. The other is to prevent the oil and moisture of human fingers from eroding the ink and parchment. Constant touching can do a lot of damage. (This is why signs in art museums say "Don't touch!")

Pointers have been used since ancient times to make sure the scrolls are handled as little as possible. Recently the custom has arisen of a bar mitzvah having his own *yad* and using it to read his portion of the text. He keeps the pointer as a remembrance of the occasion.

The Holy Ark

Torah scrolls are housed in a special cabinet called the holy ark or *aron kodesh*. A hanging lamp called the *ner tamid*, the "eternal light," hangs before the ark in memory of the lamp that burned in the tent sanctuary where the ancient Israelites worshiped during the time of Moses. This light is also a reminder of the never-ending faith of the Jewish people and of the eternal presence of God. The *ner tamid* is always kept burning. Prior to the twentieth century, the *ner tamid* was a lamp filled daily with olive oil. Today, for reasons of convenience and safety, it is nearly always an electric lamp.

A richly decorated curtain hangs before the ark. The custom of using a curtain dates back to the early history of the Jewish people. A similar curtain hung in the biblical tent sanctuary and later in the Temple in Jerusalem. In Eastern European communities, the women of the congregation sewed and embroidered the curtain as a special gift to the synagogue. This custom is regaining popularity in America. Many beautiful hangings found in synagogues today were designed and created by members of the congregation.

The Bimah

In most synagogues, the ark stands on a raised platform called the *bimah,* which is usually the size of a small stage. It has to be large enough to accommodate as many as eight people, as well as the large desk on which the Torah scroll is placed. The main activity of the synagogue service occurs on the *bimah.* This is where the Torah is read, and where the rabbi and cantor stand when addressing the congregation or leading prayers.

What Makes a Synagogue?

A synagogue can be made of wood or brick, stone or thatch, glass, marble, or steel. It can look like a bank, an *Arabian Nights* palace, a New England town hall, or a modernistic sculpture. It need not be a building at all. A tent can be a synagogue. So can a rented room, a forest clearing, or an ocean beach. A synagogue is more than a structure. Rich carvings and beautiful ornaments do not make a synagogue.

It is the people who come together for study and prayer. They are the ones who make a synagogue a true house of worship.

INTERVIEW ·····································

I wish I had happy memories of my bar mitzvah, but I don't. Even now, so many years later, I still get angry when I think about it.

It was my father's fault. I can't really blame him, but I can't forgive him either. Pop was a hard, bitter man, which isn't surprising, since he had a hard, bitter life. His parents died when he was a little boy. Whoever took him in packed him off to work when he was six years old. I only heard him say two things about his childhood. One was being hungry all the time. The second was how good the black bread in Poland tasted. There was nothing like it in America. It was probably all he got to eat. No wonder it tasted so good.

We had nine people living in our house on Pulaski Street—my parents, me and my five brothers and sisters, and our cousin Evelyn. Pop had to support nine people on a sweatshop worker's pay. He had a horror of wasting money. We never had toys or games when I was growing up. We didn't even have photographs.

My father thought providing a Jewish education for his children was an unnecessary luxury. After all, he was Jewish, and what kind of education did he have? When the time came for my bar mitzvah and he couldn't put it off any longer, he sent me over to my zayde's house. This was my mother's father. Zayde had a long beard, he prayed all the time, so my father figured he could teach me what I needed to know for my bar mitzvah. Then he wouldn't have to pay anybody.

I came over to Zayde's. He sat me down, opened up a prayer-book, and made a little speech about how wonderful it was that I was going to be bar mitzvah, what a great occasion I had to look forward to, and how proud everybody was going to be. Therefore, I must do my best and study hard, so I could learn all I needed to know. Then he started teaching me the Torah blessings. He said a word; I repeated it. He said another word; I repeated that one, too. This was my bar mitzvah preparation: Zayde saying the words one by one and me repeating them over and over again. He never explained what any of these words meant. I don't think he knew himself. All that mattered was being able to say them by heart.

After an hour of this, I looked over Zayde's shoulder to see where he was in the prayerbook. Maybe there was an English translation so I could learn what all this babble was about. That's when I got a shock. I couldn't read Hebrew, but my father got the Yiddish newspaper and there were enough signs in Yiddish and Hebrew in our neighborhood so that I was at least familiar with the shapes of the letters. I could tell when they were right side up and upside down. My pious, holy zayde with the long white beard was holding the prayerbook upside down. He couldn't read or write. He was completely illiterate. Of course he knew the prayers by heart! How could he not know them, saying them aloud every day for seventy years? But that was the way a parrot would know them—by rote. He didn't understand what he was saying or why he was saying it. He couldn't explain anything to me because he didn't know anything himself.

When I went back home, I told my father what happened.

"How is Zayde *going to teach me what I need to know for my bar mitzvah? He doesn't know anything. He was holding the prayerbook upside down. He can't even read."*

"So what!" my father shouted. "He knows the prayers. That's enough. You'll learn them from him, you'll say them when the time comes, and that will be your bar mitzvah."

And that was my bar mitzvah. I stood up at the front of the little synagogue, kissed the Torah, and mumbled the blessings. My father hosted the congregation to a little wine and cake. Very little. And that was it. I was supposed to be a Jewish adult, but I knew absolutely nothing. It was a fraud.

I have forgiven my father everything, but not that. I was proud to be Jewish. I wanted to learn. I wanted to go to a real school with real teachers. If I could have found a book that explained some things, that would have been a start. But there was nothing.

Morris N. Kimmel
Bar Mitzvah, 1923

45

THE SERVICE OF
THE HEART

···

The structure of the prayer service

May the words of my mouth and the meditations of my heart find

favor in Your sight, O Lord, my Rock and my Redeemer.
                                                    Psalms 19:15

Rabbi Moshe of Kobrin, a nineteenth-century sage who lived in
what is now Belarus, once spoke to his disciples on the subject of
prayer. He said, "Whenever you pray to God, you must enter into
each word with every part of your body."

One of his disciples asked, "How can a big human being fit
inside a little word?"

Rabbi Moshe answered, "Anyone who thinks he is bigger than
the word is not the person we are talking about."

The Rabbis referred to prayer as *avodat lev,* "the service of the heart." When Jewish people pray, they open their hearts to God. They admit their failures, their fears, their sorrows, their hopes. They plead for God's help in shielding them from misfortune and offer thanks for blessings bestowed. In the words of one famous prayer, "If our mouths were as full of song as the sea and our tongues as full of melody as the endless waves, and our lips as full of praise as the heavens, and our eyes as bright as the sun and moon, and our hands outstretched like eagle's wings, and our feet as swift as a gazelle's, we still could not thank You enough for the thousands upon thousands of favors You have bestowed upon us and our ancestors."

The Roots of Jewish Worship

The origins of Jewish worship go back more than three thousand years, to a time when the Israelites were a group of nomadic tribes wandering in the Sinai desert. At this time in Jewish history, worship centered around the *mishkan,* a portable tent sanctuary built according to specific directions in the Torah. The innermost sanctum of the *mishkan* was called the Holy of Holies. It contained a wooden chest covered with gold called the Ark of the Covenant.

Those who have seen the movie *Raiders of the Lost Ark* have a picture of what the Ark of the Covenant may have looked like, but it was certainly not the sensationalized cosmic battery depicted in that film! The Ark, which held the stone tablets of the Ten Commandments, was the most sacred object the Israelites possessed. It symbolized God's presence among the people of Israel. It made the *mishkan* a holy place. Access to the shrine was limited to priests and Levites.

Priest and Levite

The priests, or *Kohanim,* as they are called in Hebrew, were descendants of Moses' brother Aaron, the first high priest. The *Leviim*—Levites—were members of the tribe of Levi, one of the twelve tribes of Israel. Moses and Aaron were members of this tribe.

The Levites assisted the priests in performing sacrifices. They were responsible for protecting, maintaining, and transporting the *mishkan*. Although the Jewish people have not performed sacrifices for two thousand years, many Jews still preserve the lineage of priest and Levite, which is transmitted from father to son. Last names such as Cohen, Kahane, or Katz (an abbreviation for the words *Kohen tzedek,* "righteous priest") are usually indications of priestly status. Similarly, names such as Levi, Levitas, or Levine often indicate a Levite.

Although Jews have not had a high priest for two thousand years, they have preserved the memory of this imposing figure. The ornaments of the Torah and their names are taken from the high priest's garments. Its mantle, silver bells, and ornaments recall his robe and its decorations.

The high priest did not wear shoes in the *mishkan*. He and the other *Kohanim* came before God in their bare feet. In the ancient world, people took off their shoes before entering a place of worship. When Moses came upon the burning bush in the desert, God told him to remove his shoes because he was standing on holy ground. Muslims still remove their shoes before entering a mosque.

Covering the Head

With the exception of certain Sephardic congregations, Jews do not remove their shoes upon entering a synagogue. However, most men and many women cover their heads. Covering the head is considered a sign of respect; for the same reason, men remove their hats upon entering a church. Visitors to a synagogue will usually be given a skullcap to wear during the service if they don't have one. This skullcap is called a *kippah* in Hebrew (plural, *kippot*) or *yarmulke* in Yiddish (plural, *yarmulkes*).

In general, most Jewish people today cover their heads only while attending a synagogue prayer service or taking part in religious activities, such as studying holy books or participating in home observances such as the Passover seder, welcoming the Sabbath, or lighting the Hanukkah menorah. People also cover their heads for traditional blessings that precede and follow every meal. Some cover their heads only while saying these blessings. Others do so for the entire meal.

Orthodox Jewish men keep their heads covered at all times, to comply with a passage in the Talmud stating that no man should walk more than four paces with his head uncovered. The requirement to cover one's head is not mentioned in the Torah or the Mishnah. Most likely, the custom began in the Middle East, where people wore turbans and other distinctive headgear to indicate their nationality and social status. Wearing a *kippah* became a positive

badge of Jewishness, unlike the humiliating stars and special clothing that Christian and Muslim authorities sometimes forced Jews to wear. As an indication of respect, the *kippah* reminded Jews of God's presence. They kept their heads covered at all times since there was never a moment when they did not stand before God.

You can make a *kippah* of any material in any color using any design. The only rule is that it has to be big enough to cover the crown of your head. In the past, most people wore black *kippot,* with white ones reserved for holidays and special occasions. However, modern *kippot* come in astonishing varieties. They can be made of silk, suede, velvet, or leather. They can be tie-dyed, hand-painted, crocheted. You can have your name embroidered in Hebrew or English. Your *kippah* can be decorated with religious symbols, such as the menorah, the Torah scroll, or the Star of David. Or, if you prefer, you can have Super Mario, X-Men, Michael Jordan, or the Teenage Mutant Ninja Turtles.

The Temple

The portable tent sanctuary of the *mishkan* served the Israelites for two hundred years. By then they were no longer a nation of nomads. Three thousand years ago, led by David, Israel's greatest king, they captured the city of Jerusalem and made it the capital of their new kingdom.

The Bible tells how David watched the sacrifices being offered in the *mishkan* and thought, "It is not right that I should live in a palace while God dwells in a tent." He decided to build a temple, a permanent sanctuary for the worship of the God of Israel.

51

But God did not accept his offer. "You are a man of war," God told David. "My house must be a house of peace." It was David's son Solomon who received the honor of building the first Temple in Jerusalem.

There are numerous stories and legends about the building of the Temple. The most beautiful one concerns two brothers who had a threshing floor on this spot. One brother had a large family; the other lived by himself. They worked together, harvesting the wheat and threshing it. When the harvest was done, they divided the grain equally.

That night, as the brother who lived alone stored the grain in his barn, he thought, "My brother has a large family to feed, while I have only myself. I don't need all this grain. I will bring some to my brother." He filled several sacks with grain, loaded them on his donkey, and set out for his brother's house in the dead of night.

Meanwhile, his brother was storing his grain in his barn. He thought, "Is it really fair that my brother and I should have equal shares of this grain? My brother worked much harder than I did. He had to harvest his portion of the field by himself. I had seven strong sons to help me. My brother toiled all alone. I have more than enough grain for my family's needs. I will give some to my brother. He is entitled to a larger share." He filled several sacks with grain, loaded them on his donkey, and set out for his brother's house.

The brothers met at the threshing floor. As the moon shined down, each looked at the other with surprise.

"Where are you going with that grain?"

"I am bringing it to you. You are entitled to a larger share."

"On the contrary, I think you are entitled to a larger share. That is why I am bringing this grain to you!"

The two brothers fell into each other's arms, laughing and weeping, for their hearts were filled with love. God looked down from heaven and said, "I will build my Temple on the place where these two brothers showed their love for each other. My house, too, will be a house of love, and a house of peace."

The Western Wall

By all accounts, Solomon's Temple was a splendid building. Thirty thousand Israelites took part in its construction, along with one hundred and fifty thousand laborers of other nations.

Solomon dedicated the Temple in 958 B.C.E. It stood until 587 B.C.E., when it was destroyed by the Babylonians during the siege of Jerusalem. Rebuilt in 512 B.C.E., it was later enlarged and expanded by Herod, a Jewish king appointed by the Romans to rule Judea. This is the same Herod mentioned in the New Testament. The Judeans detested him for his violence and cruelty. Herod hoped to increase his popularity by making the Temple one of the most beautiful buildings in the world. He succeeded in that, but it didn't help his image. He was hated as much as ever. Even so, Herod was a shrewd politician. He knew how far he could push his subjects without sparking a rebellion. The Roman governors who followed him weren't as astute. Their misrule sparked a revolution that led to the destruction of Jerusalem and the Temple in 70 C.E. The Mosque of Omar currently occupies the spot where the Temple stood.

Few traces of Solomon's Temple remain. However, some remnants of Herod's structure still stand. The best known of these is the *kotel ha'maaravi,* the Western Wall, or Wailing Wall, as it is sometimes called.

The wall acquired this name from generations of Jewish pilgrims who came to the site to mourn the loss of the Temple. Those who came to pray at the *kotel* would frequently write little notes to God, and wedge these among the ancient stones. Since the wall had been part of the Holy Temple, people felt that prayers or requests made here would find special favor. It is interesting, and sometimes amusing, to note how modern technology can be used to expand upon age-old religious customs. A fax machine was recently set up at the *kotel* so that notes to God can now be faxed in from all over the world.

When the Old City of Jerusalem came under Jordanian rule in 1948, Jewish access to the *kotel* ended. Over the next nineteen years, the Jordanians leveled centuries-old synagogues and bulldozed ancient cemeteries in an effort to erase all traces of Jewish presence in the Old City. No Jew could visit the *kotel* until 1967, when a reunited Jerusalem came under Israeli rule after the Six-Day War. The *kotel* once again became a major site of pilgrimage. Because of its significance in Jewish history, hundreds of bar mitzvah celebrations take place there every year.

The Temple is more than a historical footnote. Several important elements of the modern synagogue service were originally part of the Temple ritual. These include the priestly blessing, the Psalms, the *Shema* prayer— which begins with the famous words "Hear, O Israel, the Lord our God, the Lord is One"—two daily services, and *musaf,* the additional service on Sabbaths, New Moons, and Festivals.

The Rise of the Synagogue

The Torah required all male Israelites to come before the Lord three times a year, at the festivals of Passover, Shavuot, and Sukkot. Once the Temple was built, thousands of people made the pilgrimage to Jerusalem.

The destruction of the First Temple in 587 B.C.E. created a religious crisis. Since sacrifices could be offered only at the Temple, the central act of Jewish worship came to an abrupt end. It was no longer possible to worship God in the way prescribed by the Torah. Worst of all, most of the Jewish population was taken into exile in Babylonia. This is how the Diaspora—the separation of the Jews from the land of Israel—began. This might have led to the end of the Jewish people. Other more powerful nations, such as the Assyrians, the Hittites, and the Babylonians themselves, disappeared after their countries were conquered and their people dispersed.

This did not happen to the Jewish people. Instead of forsaking the Torah and adopting the customs of the Babylonians, Jews persisted in preserving their national identity. They could no longer offer sacrifices, but on Sabbaths and festivals, they gathered together at the home of a respected local leader. These leaders encouraged people to continue following the teachings of the Torah. They kept alive the promise that God would one day bring the Jews back to the land of Israel, where sacrifices would be offered once again in a new, restored Temple.

Over the years, these informal prayer gatherings evolved into a revolutionary form of worship: that of the synagogue. The Torah scroll, in place of the Holy of Holies, came to be regarded as the physical sign of God's presence. For the first time in the Western world, people conceived the idea that a worshiper could experience closeness to God without killing an animal. Prayer and study began to be considered as important as sacrifices.

The synagogue quickly became a major force in Jewish life, especially after the destruction of the Second Temple in 70 C.E. Jews never gave up the hope that the Temple might be restored, but slowly the feeling began to grow that God valued a pure heart more than sacrifices, and that sincere devotion and ethical conduct were more pleasing to Him than burnt offerings. In the words of the Prophet Micah:

"What does the Lord ask of you? Act justly, love mercy, and walk humbly with your God." (Micah 6:8)

Rabbis and Teachers

The rise of the synagogue democratized the Jewish religion and made it more responsive to the needs and concerns of ordinary people. Any group of ten men over the age of thirteen could form a synagogue. Unlike priests and Levites, who inherited their status from their fathers, a religious leader could be any man willing to devote himself to studying the Torah and following its teachings. Such a leader was called a rav or rabbi. Judaism passed this tradition on to Christianity and Islam. Spiritual authority in all three religions derives from piety and learning.

Rabbi Yochanan's Daring Escape

The destruction of the Second Temple and the devastation of the Holy Land by the Romans was a calamity not only for the Jews living in Israel, but for all the Jewish people scattered throughout the world. Its impact might have been fatal if the institution of the synagogue had not existed to cushion the blow. Almost immediately after the fall of Jerusalem, a group of scholars assembled in the seacoast town of Yavneh under the leadership of a heroic leader, Rabbi Yochanan ben Zakkai.

Rabbi Yochanan's story has all the elements of a great movie: violence, intrigue, a daring escape, and ultimately, a happy ending.

Rabbi Yochanan had opposed the revolt against the Romans. He told his disciples, "It is folly to start a war with the greatest military power on earth. The Romans will crush us. As to those who say that God will give His people the victory, I say His people would be better off to pray and study and work for peace."

Needless to say, Rabbi Yochanan was not popular with the armed zealots who had taken over Jerusalem. With the siege of Jerusalem at its height and with famine and disease taking more lives every day, he begged to be allowed to go out of the city to work out a peace treaty with the Romans. The Jewish commanders refused. No one was allowed to leave.

Rabbi Yochanan realized that the survival of the Jewish people was at stake. He worked out a daring plan to rescue a remnant of the people for the future. He told his disciples to give out the word that he had died. They placed Rabbi Yochanan in a coffin and asked for permission to bury him outside the walls. Permission was granted.

Once outside the city, Rabbi Yochanan hurried to the Roman camp. Vespasian, the Roman general soon to become emperor, greeted him warily.

"I know you have always spoken out for peace between Rome and Judea," Vespasian said.

"If I am worthy of favor in the eyes of Rome, grant me one request. Spare the city."

"I cannot do that unless its leaders surrender, and you know they never will," Vespasian answered.

"Then at least allow the women and children, the old and the sick, to leave."

The Roman general shook his head.

Finally Rabbi Yochanan asked, "Grant me this request and I will ask for nothing more. When this terrible war is over, allow me to establish a school in the town of Yavneh."

Vespasian granted this seemingly harmless request—and unwittingly ensured the survival of the Jewish people.

Coping with Crisis

The most pressing challenge facing the Rabbis who gathered with Yochanan ben Zakkai at Yavneh was how to deal with the fact that sacrifices could no longer be offered. They solved this problem by declaring that *tefilah* (prayer), *Torah* (study), and *mitzvot* (good deeds) were as acceptable to God as sacrifices. *Avodah,* the Temple sacrifice, was replaced by *avodat lev,* the service of the heart—at least until the Temple would be rebuilt.

The Rabbis of Yavneh were religious revolutionaries, but they did not think of themselves as such. In their own eyes, they were practical men trying to cope with a crisis. They never abandoned the idea of the Temple. On the contrary, they expected it to be restored eventually, as had happened in the past. To prepare for that day and to make sure the Temple ritual was not forgotten, they incorporated as much of that ritual as possible into the synagogue service.

It was also necessary to preserve the lineage of *Kohen* and *Levi* for the day when the Temple would be restored and the priests and Levites would resume their age-old duties. To achieve this, *Kohanim* and *Leviim* were given special roles that in many synagogues continue down to the present day. The honor of reading the first Torah portion is reserved for a *Kohen,* if one is present. The second portion is given to a *Levi.* On Sabbaths and festivals the *Kohanim* in the congregation are called on to pronounce the priestly blessing, just as their ancestors did at the time when the Temple stood.

The Rabbis of Yavneh established another important principle: Reading a description of a sacrifice has the same merit as actually performing it. Passages describing the sacrifices offered on Sabbaths or festivals, and for daily worship were taken from the Torah and included among the prayers. Descriptions of the ancient Temple sacrifices can still be found in prayerbooks used by Orthodox and Conservative congregations.

An Ancient Hope

It has been almost two thousand years since the Temple stood in Jerusalem. The thought of worshiping God by killing animals and burning their bodies would strike most people today—including most Jews—as barbaric. Yet the hope for a restored Temple lingers on in parts of the Jewish liturgy.

More important, the essence of Temple worship survives in the synagogue. Whether Orthodox, Conservative, or Reform, Ashkenazic or Sephardic, Jews still find their deepest hopes expressed in the words once spoken by the high priest when he stretched his arms out over the people and invoked the age-old blessing:

May the Lord bless you and keep you.
May the Lord let His face shine upon you and be gracious unto you.
May the Lord lift up His countenance unto you and give you peace.

INTERVIEW ··

Do you know that becoming bar mitzvah can be hazardous to your health? It's true. I had a near-fatal accident at mine.

I grew up in Jerusalem, in Israel. All the synagogues there are Orthodox. Men and women don't sit together. In my synagogue, the women and little kids sat upstairs in a separate balcony. When a boy becomes bar mitzvah, it's the custom to shower him with candy and sweets from the balcony.

When I finished chanting my haftarah, the reading from the

Prophets, they started throwing down the candy. I think one of those women must have really taken aim and thrown hard. This candy came at me like a bullet, or like that rock David threw at Goliath. It hit me in the forehead, right between the eyes. I nearly fell down on the bimah, *and I had to go through my whole bar mitzvah with a big lump on my head. It wasn't funny.*

So my advice to anyone who is going to have a bar mitzvah in a place where they have this candy-throwing custom is—don't wear a kippah. *Wear a helmet.*

Hanoch Livneh
Bar Mitzvah, 1963

TORAH AND HAFTARAH

The Torah ritual and the bar mitzvah ceremony

The Torah is a Tree of Life for those who cling to it, and those who

support it are fortunate.

From the prayer book

According to the Torah, God promised Abraham that his descendants would be as numerous as the sands of the sea and the stars in the sky. The Rabbis questioned these words. They asked, "Would it not be sufficient to say 'as numerous as the sands of the sea' or 'as numerous as the stars in the sky'? Why does the Torah use both?"

The answer they gave is that God showed Abraham a vision of his future offspring. He saw that the Jewish people would often be persecuted and downtrodden like sand on the seashore. But in the end, God would raise them up to be like the stars in the heavens.

To become bar mitzvah is to become part of Abraham's vision. Sometimes being Jewish means being a grain of sand, rolled and pummeled by waves, battered by storms. Yet every one of those grains of sand rejoices in the hope that in the end it will become a shining star.

Preparations for a bar mitzvah ceremony begin long before a boy's thirteenth birthday. Few synagogues or temples in the United States allow a bar mitzvah ceremony to take place unless the boy has attended religious school for several years or can otherwise demonstrate knowledge of Jewish history, ethics, and practice, as well as a basic familiarity with the Hebrew language.

The Hebrew words *bar mitzvah* mean "one who has the obligation of fulfilling a *mitzvah*." The word *mitzvah* and its plural, *mitzvot,* refer to the commandments that God gave to the Jewish people when Moses received the Torah on Mount Sinai. In other words, becoming bar mitzvah means that one is prepared to function as a Jewish adult. The community recognizes this fact by inviting the bar mitzvah to do something which an immature child is not permitted to do: participate in, or even lead, the Torah service.

The Torah Service

In traditional synagogues that hold daily services, the Torah is read four times a week, on Monday and Thursday and twice on Saturday (at morning and afternoon services). According to legend, Moses instituted the practice of reading the Torah on these days so that no more than three days would go by without at least a minimum of Torah study. There were also practical reasons for choosing these days. Monday and Thursday were market days, when people from outlying areas would come into town to trade. Saturday is, of course, the Sabbath, when people have time to sit and listen. Most bar mitzvah ceremonies take place on the Sabbath.

The Torah readings for Monday, Thursday, and Saturday afternoon are fairly short. However, the one on Saturday morning is an impressive ritual. It is the climax of the Sabbath service.

The Torah reading occurs in the middle of the Sabbath service, after the main prayers and before the *musaf,* the additional service. The ark is opened, and the congregation stands as the Torah scroll is lifted out. With its polished silver ornaments shining and their tiny bells ringing, the Torah is carried around the synagogue while the congregation sings a rousing hymn, "To you, O God, belong the greatness, power, glory...." Members of the congregation touch the scroll with their prayer books or the corners of their prayer shawls, which they will then kiss as the Torah goes by, since "kissing the Torah" is an act of special love and respect. The Torah is carried back up to the *bimah,* the raised platform where the Torah reading will take place. After its ornaments and mantle are removed, the scroll is laid on the reading desk, untied, and opened to the portion that is going to be read. The congregation sits and the Torah reading begins.

Reading the Torah

The practice of reading from the Torah goes back to at least the fourth century B.C.E. when the priest Ezra led the exiles back to Israel from Babylon. Reading a religious book aloud was a revolutionary idea for its time. The priests of other religions jealously guarded their sacred texts. Only priests or those studying to be priests could read them. In fact, few other people could read at all. The word *hieroglyphic,* used to describe the picture writing of the ancient Egyptians, means "priestly writing."

Every Jew, however, could hear the Torah read aloud in the synagogue, from beginning to end. God's word was not the special property of a small group. It belonged to the entire Jewish people, and was read aloud and explained so that all could hear and understand.

Anyone who speaks or reads Hebrew can follow the words of the Torah without a translation. Biblical Hebrew is three thousand years old, but it is not too different from the Hebrew spoken in Israel today. The language of the Torah may seem old-fashioned to a modern Israeli, but understanding it is no more difficult for one of them than it is for the average American to listen to one of Shakespeare's plays. However, being a *baal korei,* the official reader at a synagogue service, is another matter. That requires considerable practice and study.

No Vowels!

Th Hbrw lngg ws rgnll wrttn wtht vwls. (The Hebrew language was originally written without vowels.) This is how the words in a Torah scroll are written: consonants only. (Hebrew letters are written and read from right to left.) Unlike *a, e, i, o, u* and *y* in English, Hebrew vowels are not separate letters. They are marks that are written below, beside, and above the consonants. To give an idea of how this works, the letter bet has the *b* sound. Dots and lines are vowels that give the sounds *ee, ah,* and *eh.* The letter bet can thus be pronounced *bee, bah,* or *beh,* depending on which vowel is placed beneath it.

Vowels are included in printed versions of the Torah, but they are not used in writing a scroll. This is because written representations of the Hebrew vowel system came into use sometime between the sixth and eighth centuries, long after the official text of the Torah had been established. Since a scribe is not permitted to add anything to a Torah (or leave anything out), the scrolls do not contain vowels. Nor, for the same reason, do they have any punctuation.

It might be assumed that reading from a Torah scroll is extremely difficult. Imagine reading this book without benefit of paragraphs, commas, periods, or vowels. Actually, it is not as impossible as it seems. In some ways, it is like learning to read a musical score. An experienced reader familiar with the Hebrew language and the text of the Torah knows by study, context, and memory how to pronounce the words and how to read the sentences. However, it is always possible to make a mistake. Since a misplaced vowel can alter the entire meaning of a word or sentence, someone always follows along in a printed text with the vowels and punctuation added, to make sure the reader, the *baal korei,* is reading the Torah accurately.

As if that weren't enough, the *baal korei* doesn't merely read the words of the portion. He sings them, using centuries-old melodies. The notes and combinations of notes that go with each word were devised hundreds of years before the development of standard musical notation. The melody is indicated by special marks written above and below the words, just like the vowels. These notations aren't written in the Torah scroll either, although they are included in the printed text. The reader, however, has to know the chant by heart when he reads from the scroll. That is why being able to read the Torah requires considerable study.

Portions of the Week

The Torah text is divided into fifty-four sections called *parshiyot* or "portions," which are named after the first significant word in the first sentence. In traditional synagogues, the *parshiyot* are read in consecutive order, one *parashah* at each Sabbath service. Thus the entire Torah is read in the course of a year.

Wait a minute! Since there are fifty-two weeks in a year and fifty-four *parshiyot,* wouldn't that leave two extra Torah readings? It would, which is why occasionally two *parshiyot* are combined.

At one time, the Torah reading followed a triennial cycle. This was the custom in Israel at the time of the Talmud. The Torah was variously divided into either 153, 155, or 167 *parshiyot*. The full text was read in the course of three years. The annual cycle eventually became standard, but even as late as the twelfth century, the three-year cycle continued to be followed in some places. Some contemporary congregations have partially revived this custom by reading one third of the weekly *parashah*. The advantage? It makes for a considerably shorter Torah reading. Some Reform congregations select the verses for the weekly reading from different portions of the *parashah,* instead of starting at the beginning. There are even a few instances of congregations reviving the full three-year cycle, although this is less common.

The *parashah* that is read at the Sabbath service is usually divided into seven parts, since tradition requires seven different people to read at least ten verses each for the Torah reading to be valid. Originally people called up to the Torah read their portions themselves. This is still the custom in some synagogues. However, most synagogues use a professional reader, the *baal korei,* who reads for everyone. In this way, even those who are unable to read the *parashah* can still take part in the Torah service.

The Honor of Aliyah

The honor of being called to the Torah is called an *aliyah.* The word means "to go up." In all Orthodox and some Conservative congregations, *aliyot* are reserved for men and boys who are past the age of bar mitzvah. The first two go to a *Kohen* and a *Levi* if any are present. However, less orthodox congregations don't follow this practice. Many extend the honor of an *aliyah* to women as well as men.

The person called for an *aliyah* stands before the reading desk next to the *baal korei.* Using the *yad* so as not to touch the Torah with bare fingers, the *baal korei* indicates the place where the *parashah* begins. The person given the *aliyah* touches the corner of his prayer shawl to the first word, kisses it, and then, grasping the Torah scroll's wooden handles, chants the following:

"Barchu et Adonai ha'mevorach."

(May you all bless the Lord, the blessed One.)

The congregation responds:

"Baruch Adonai ha'mevorach l'olam va'ed."

(Blessed be the Lord for all eternity.)

The person given the *aliyah* repeats these words and continues in Hebrew:

"Blessed be the Lord for all eternity. Blessed are You, Lord, our God, Ruler of the universe, who has chosen us from all other nations to give us His Torah. Blessed are You, Lord, who has given the Torah."

The congregation responds, "Amen." The person given the *aliyah* stands aside and the *baal korei* begins reading the *parashah* from the Torah scroll, using the *yad* as a pointer. The congregation follows the reading in their copies of the printed version of the Torah, where the text is supplemented with notes and an English translation. When the *baal korei* finishes, he indicates the stopping place to the person given the *aliyah,* who kisses the Torah once more, then chants in Hebrew:

"Blessed are You, Lord, our God, Ruler of the universe, who has given us the Torah's truth and so planted eternal life in our midst. Blessed are You, Lord, who gives the Torah."

The person with the second *aliyah* is called and the Torah reading continues.

After the person receiving the seventh *aliyah* finishes, the *baal korei* calls an eighth person to the Torah. This is the *maftir*—"the one who concludes." The *maftir* will read the haftarah, a selection from the writings of the Prophets, after the Torah reading is over. If there is a boy who is celebrating his bar mitzvah that day, this honor traditionally goes to him. Reform congregations usually omit having a special *aliyah* for the *maftir*. At the end of the Torah reading, two members of the congregation are called up to receive the honors of *magbehah* ("lifter") and *golel* ("roller").

Lifting the Torah

As the congregation rises, the *magbehah* takes hold of the scroll by its two bottom handles and unrolls it enough to show at least three columns of text. He turns around and lifts it up so that everyone in the synagogue can see the words written on the parchment. A large Torah scroll can weigh twenty pounds or more. Lifting one is like hoisting two barbells by their ends. This makes the honor of being the *magbehah* one of the few in Judaism that require more strength than learning.

There is a lovely anecdote that has to do with the weight of a Torah scroll. A fine new Torah was once dedicated at the synagogue of Rabbi David Moshe of Chortkov. As the rabbi lifted it, his disciples became alarmed because David Moshe was so frail and the scroll was so heavy. They tried to take it from him, but the rabbi said, "Once you hold it, it isn't heavy anymore."

As the *magbehah* lifts the Torah, the congregation sings in Hebrew:

"This is the Torah which Moses set before the Children of Israel, according to God's word as given to Moses."

After showing the Torah to the congregation, the *magbehah* sits down with it. The *golel* rolls up the scroll, ties it, and replaces the mantle and other ornaments. In some congregations, the *magbehah* will hold the scroll while seated, until the Torah service ends.

The Haftarah

People resume their seats. Only the *maftir* remains standing as the haftarah portion of the service begins.

The practice of including a selection from the writings of the Prophets to complement the Torah reading goes back to at least the second century C.E. The fixed selections from the Prophets that are read with each *parashah* today were not fixed until about a thousand years ago. Before that time, even as early as the third century B.C.E., it was customary for a scholar attending the Sabbath service to be invited to deliver a *Dvar Torah,* a sermon based on the Torah reading. As part of his lesson, he would read a selection from the prophetical writings and explain how it was related to the *parashah*. He was free to choose whatever he felt was appropriate.

An episode in the New Testament illustrates this practice. Luke 4:16–30 describes how Jesus once attended a Sabbath service at a synagogue in Nazareth. After reading the Torah portion, he was handed a scroll containing the Book of Isaiah. Jesus read from the scroll and proceeded to address the congregation.

What occurred in Nazareth two thousand years ago still happens in most synagogues today. A boy celebrating his bar mitzvah reads from the Torah, then chants the haftarah, and in some instances delivers a sermon, a *Dvar Torah,* based on the two.

The *maftir* begins his reading with a blessing praising God for giving Israel the Torah and truthful, righteous prophets. He then proceeds to chant the haftarah. The chant used for the haftarah is different from that of the Torah reading, but the *maftir* has a some-what easier task than the *baal korei.* He is permitted to read from a printed text that includes vowels and musical notation. The members of the congregation follow the haftarah reading in Hebrew or in English translation.

These age-old selections are extremely moving, especially when they are considered in the context of the previous Torah reading. For example, the haftarah that goes with the story of Noah and the great flood is a selection from the Book of Isaiah that opens with the image of a childless wife being promised a joyous household full of children. While the haftarah contains a brief reference to Noah's flood (Isaiah 54:9), its connection with the Torah reading goes far beyond that. After the destruction of the Temple and the removal of the Jewish people from the land of Israel to exile in Babylonia, the prophet exhorts the exiles not to abandon hope. He assures them that God has not forgotten them. God's love for Israel remains unchanging and the covenant still stands. He gives them the promise that God will restore them to their land, in greater joy and glory than they have ever known. The image of the flood's destruction and the rainbow of God's promise in the *parashah* is mirrored in the image of the destruc-tion of Jerusalem and the promised redemption in the haftarah.

The *Maftir* Blessings

After completing the haftarah, the *maftir* recites four long blessings. Reform Jews usually use an abbreviated form; Orthodox and Conservative Jews will recite all four. The first blessing praises God, Whose words are filled with righteousness and truth. The second asks for a speedy return to Zion, the land of Israel. The third is a prayer for the coming of Elijah the prophet and the restoration of the royal House of David and the kingdom of Israel. The fourth and last is a prayer of thanks for the blessings of the Torah, the Prophets, and the Sabbath day of rest.

The recitation of the haftarah is followed by special prayers for teachers, rabbis, and their students, as well as for those who support synagogues and community organizations. There is a prayer for the nation's government and its leaders. Some congregations also include a prayer for the leaders of the State of Israel and express a hope for peace.

The Torah portion of the Sabbath service closes with the recitation of Psalms. The scrolls are then carried around the synagogue in a joyous procession before being replaced in the ark. If the boy celebrating his bar mitzvah has prepared a *Dvar Torah,* he will give it at this time. If not, the rabbi will deliver a sermon, usually based on some aspect of the week's Torah reading or haftarah, or on a topic of importance to the community. This is followed by the *musaf* service and a memorial prayer called the *Kaddish,* or Sanctification, offered in memory of members of the congregation and their relatives who have passed away. The Sabbath service concludes with the singing of hymns.

• BAR MITZVAH •

Obviously, anyone preparing for a bar mitzvah has a lot to learn. The ceremony itself takes less than an hour. Getting ready for it takes an entire year.

INTERVIEW ···

Preparing for my bar mitzvah was a challenge. My father is a prominent rabbi. His friends are rabbis and Jewish scholars, brilliant men, who know the Torah and Talmud inside out. These were the people who were coming to my bar mitzvah. Do you think that's intimidating? Let me tell you: It is!

My father had big plans. I was going to read the whole parashah *and do the* maftir. *That's asking a lot, but I agreed. Then, on top of that, he wanted me to give a* Dvar Torah, *a learned address on some aspect of the* parashah. *That's when I put my foot down. No way was I going to do that! I knew my father's friends wouldn't laugh at me, but how could he expect the greatest Jewish scholars in the world to take a lecture from a thirteen-year-old seriously!*

I was extremely nervous, even though I had an excellent teacher who prepared me well. I don't think I stopped shaking until I got to the seventh aliyah. *Suddenly my nervousness disappeared. I thought, "You've come this far. You're nearly done. You can do it." I relaxed and began to enjoy the experience.*

If you can believe this, my father also wanted me to do another haftarah *reading on Sunday at the reception. I did the Ashkenazic reading on Saturday. This was one of those Sabbaths where*

76

the Sephardim read a different haftarah. My father wanted me to do both on Sunday, just to show I could do it. I guess it's like a father who was a football star in college wanting to see his son score the winning touchdown for his high school team. Too bad! Becoming bar mitzvah once is tough enough. I wasn't about to do it twice.

Daniel Finkelstein
Bar Mitzvah, 1994

INTERVIEW ··

My bar mitzvah experience was different from most. My parents went to a synagogue that encouraged children to take part in the service. So from the time I was five or six, I was accustomed to being called up to the Torah for an aliyah. *Reading the Torah looked interesting, so I learned how to do it. I was reading from the Torah from the time I was seven years old. I liked it. It was a challenge and a thrill. These were God's actual words, and I had to read them correctly because the slightest mistake can change the meaning completely. Once you know how to read the Torah, a haftarah is easy.*

I didn't really have a teacher for my bar mitzvah. By then I had been reading the parshiyot *and* haftarot *for years. Someone checked on me every month or so, to make sure I was on the right track and not making any mistakes. But I guess you can say I taught myself.*

I did have one problem. The synagogue I went to was on the triennial cycle. They take three years to finish reading the Torah instead of one. That means the weekly portions are smaller. But I wanted to do the full parashah *with all seven* aliyot. *They wouldn't allow that. I can understand why. There's always a little competition involved in these things. If I did it, then somebody else would want to do it, and so on. So my mother said, "Let's find another synagogue." That's what we did.*

That's where we go now. And that's where I'm still reading the Torah, just about every week.

Jesse Rodin
Bar Mitzvah, 1991

TALLIT AND TEFILLIN

Ritual objects associated with the bar mitzvah ceremony

Let these words which I teach you today be in your heart. Teach them to your children, and speak of them when you sit in your house, when you walk by the wayside, when you lie down and when you rise up. Bind them as a sign on your arm, and let them be a symbol upon your forehead. Write them upon the doorposts of your house, and upon your gates.

Deuteronomy 6: 6–9

In some families, it is customary for the parents to give their son two special gifts before his bar mitzvah.

The Prayer Shawl

The first gift is a *tallit* (plural, *tallitot*), a prayer shawl. The *tallit* is a garment traditionally worn by Jewish males during weekday, Sabbath, and festival morning services. On only one occasion is it worn in the evening: at the Kol Nidre service on the eve of Yom Kippur, the Day of Atonement, the holiest day in the Jewish calendar, when Jews reflect on their past actions and aspire to do better in the year that is to come.

Customs vary as to when a person begins wearing a *tallit*. Orthodox and Conservative congregations expect married men to wear a *tallit* during worship services. They provide *tallitot* for visitors who do not bring their own. Wearing the *tallit* is optional in most Reform congregations. In some congregations, women may also wear a *tallit* if they choose.

Tallitot vary in size. The minimum length is one that would cover a small child and still permit him to walk. The largest ones are as big as blankets, reaching from the head to just above the ankles. A *tallit* should be at least a handbreadth shorter than the garment underneath it, to make sure it doesn't drag on the ground.

A *tallit* is one of a Jew's dearest possessions. He will wrap himself in it each morning when he prays, and he will be wrapped in it one last time when he dies. It is a symbol of God's love and blessing, enfolding those who worship Him.

An incident from the fifteenth century gives an idea of the preciousness of a *tallit*. In 1493, the Jews of Sicily were ordered to leave the island. They were allowed to take nothing with them. Everything they owned had to be left behind. The elders of the community begged the authorities for one favor. They didn't ask for money to help them start new lives or food to sustain them on the sea voyage. They only asked that each Jewish man be allowed to take his *tallit*.

The word *tallit* means "cloak" or "gown." Its origins go back to the beginnings of the Jewish people, when men wore a rectangular outergarment made of wool or linen. A similar garment called an *abbayah* is still worn by Bedouin tribes throughout the Middle East today. In ancient times, distinguished Greeks and Romans wore a square-cut mantle made of fine wool. This garment, called a *pallium* or *toga,* was a mark of official status and personal distinction. Rabbis and scholars adapted this custom and took to wearing finely woven *tallitot* when presiding over worship or study sessions. In the course of time, the *tallit* lost its original function as a cloak for cold or rainy weather and became a religious garment. However, the *tallit* itself is much less important than the fringes attached to its four corners.

The Four Fringes

According to the Torah, God instructed Moses to tell the Israelites to attach a special fringe to the four corners of their outer garments. This fringe, which actually looks more like a tassel, is called a *tzitzit* (plural, *tzitziyot*). A tallit has four *tzitziyot,* one in each corner. The *tzitziyot* are worn as a reminder to keep the Torah's commandments.

The Rabbis attached great importance to wearing the *tzitzit*. They explained the reason for these special fringes by pointing out that the servants of a great lord always wore their master's badge or some type of mark on their clothing to indicate whom they served. God commanded the Jewish people to wear the *tzitzit* for the same reason—as a constant reminder to themselves and others that they are servants of the God of Israel. The Rabbis considered the *tzitzit* to be a powerful shield against immorality, since a person would surely think twice about breaking the Torah's commandments with these holy symbols attached to his clothing.

The Sky-Blue Thread

The Torah commandment concerning *tzitzit* requires that *tzitziyot* contain "a sky-blue thread." The word used for "blue" is *tekhelet*. *Tekhelet* was a special dye extracted from the bodies of deepwater sea snails that live offshore in the eastern Mediterranean. The dye came in different shades, ranging from blue to green to purple.

Tekhelet was expensive. The snails used to make it are not easily caught, and large numbers of them are required to make even a small amount of dye. A modern researcher discovered that it took twelve thousand snails to make 1.4 grams of dye, about as much as four aspirin tablets. Purple was the costliest shade. Kings wore purple robes to show their wealth and power. Consequently, the color purple became associated with royalty. To this day, the expression "born to the purple" refers to someone destined to rule over others.

The Talmud indicates that *tekhelet* continued to be manufactured until about fifteen hundred years ago. After that, the secret for making the dye was lost and no more could be obtained.

Tallitot no longer contain fringes with the blue thread. However, in honor of the commandment, *tallitot* are traditionally woven with blue or black stripes. The two horizontal blue stripes in the flag of modern Israel come from the *tallit,* which bears them in memory of the *tekhelet* thread that marked the Israelites's dedication to God.

Making a *Tallit*

Tallitot have been sober garments for most of Jewish history. However, recent years have seen an explosion of *tallitot* in exciting colors and patterns. Traditionalists may find a blue *tallit* with gold stripes unsettling, but there is nothing in the Torah that forbids it. A *tallit* can be any color or combination of colors. It can be made of wool, silk, or an artificial fiber such as rayon. The only restrictions are that the *tzitziyot* must be made of the same material, unless they are made of wool (wool *tzitziyot* can be used with any *tallit*), and that it have an *atarah,* a band at the top part which is draped over the neck.

Making your own *tallit* can be an interesting challenge. It is not difficult. The simplest way is to attach woolen *tzitziyot* to the corners of an attractive blanket or tablecloth. The Israeli flag with the Jewish star, the Magen David, in the middle, makes an unusual, but certainly "kosher" *tallit*. Skilled craftspeople have created striking *tallitot*. Sometimes, they not only design and weave the *tallit,* but also raise and shear the sheep, card and dye the wool, and spin it by hand. This may seem like a modern innovation, but it is exactly how a *tallit* was made in the days of the Bible.

Putting on a *Tallit*

Once one has acquired a *tallit,* it is important to know what to do with it. A boy preparing for his bar mitzvah celebration will already know how to put on a *tallit* if he has been attending Sabbath services regularly. Nonetheless, his teacher will probably review the rules for him. Before putting on the *tallit,* he should untangle the *tzitziyot* and examine the threads to make sure they are not torn. If a *tzitzit* is damaged, the *tallit* cannot be worn until it is replaced.

Holding the *tallit* horizontally at shoulder height, he says the following blessing in Hebrew:

"Blessed are You, Lord, our God, Ruler of the universe, who has sanctified us with Your commandments and commanded us to wrap ourselves in the *tallit*."

Various rules govern the wearing of the *tallit*. What is important to remember is that the *tallit* is a religious garment. It should always be treated with the respect it deserves.

Tefillin

The second gift some parents give their son before his bar mitzvah celebration is a pair of tefillin. Tefillin are small black leather boxes containing four sets of verses from the Torah written on parchment. The two boxes are secured with leather straps which are also painted black on the outside. The "tefillin of the hand" is

usually worn on the bicep of the left arm opposite the heart. The "tefillin of the head" is worn above the forehead with the edge extending no further than the hairline.

The regular use of tefillin is a distinctive feature of traditional Jewish worship. Tefillin are worn during daily morning prayers by men and boys of bar mitzvah age or older. They are not worn on festivals or Sabbaths, when most bar mitzvah ceremonies take place. Reform Jews rarely wear tefillin. Unless a person attends a daily morning service at an Orthodox or Conservative synagogue, it is unlikely that he or she will ever see tefillin used.

This is unfortunate, because tefillin, like the *tallit,* are rich in religious symbolism. Rabbi Moses ben Nachman, a medieval Spanish scholar and mystic, explained the significance of tefillin by saying that we place one box upon the arm to remind us of God's outstretched arm, which saves and protects His people Israel, as it did in ages past. The other box is placed upon the head, above the brain, as a reminder that intelligence, emotions, and senses, all of which are housed in the brain, must be subject to God's will.

"A Sign upon Your Arm and a Symbol Between Your Eyes"

There is some disagreement as to what the word *tefillin* really means. It appears to be related to *tefilah,* the Hebrew word for "prayer." Tefillin are put on after the *tallit,* at the start of the morning prayer service. According to Jewish tradition, the practice of wearing tefillin goes back to biblical times. However, the plain fact is that tefillin, unlike *tzitzit,* are not specifically mentioned in the Torah. What the Torah does say is, "These words shall be a sign upon your hand and a reminder between your eyes." (Exodus 13:9) This commandment has always been interpreted literally. The head and the arm tefillin each contain biblical passages written on parchment. Thus, when a person puts on tefillin, he literally binds these words around his arm and places them on his forehead between his eyes.

Like the *tallit,* tefillin are put on standing up. Several Hebrew blessings accompany each stage of putting on the head and hand tefillin, concluding with these words from the Book of Hosea (Hosea 19–20):

"I will betroth you to Myself forever. I will betroth you to Myself in righteousness and justice and in love and in mercy. I will betroth you to Myself in faithfulness, so that you will know the Lord."

These are the same words used in the Jewish wedding ceremony when bride and groom pledge themselves to each other. According to the rabbis, one should pledge oneself to God the same way, out of love and devotion.

At the end of the morning service, tefillin are removed and put back into the embroidered bag in which they are stored. The *tallit* is folded, and the *tzitzityot* are tucked inside, and it, too, is replaced in its bag. Like *kippot,* these bags were traditionally made of blue or black velvet with a touch of embroidery. Now they can be found in all sorts of fabrics, decorated with beautiful patterns and bright colors.

In times past, the act of putting on tefillin for the first time was a major event in a boy's life. This occasion took place several weeks before his bar mitzvah celebration. The boy would accompany his father to the synagogue. His father would instruct him in the rules concerning tefillin and assist him in putting them on. In Sephardic communities, a boy's first putting on tefillin called for a special celebration almost as important as the bar mitzvah celebration itself.

God's Tefillin

As might be expected with such important ritual objects, there are many folktales and legends about the *tallit* and tefillin: they protect against sin and death; they ward off evil spirits; they help overcome trials and dangers. Two especially moving tales concern Rabbi Levi Yitzhak of Berdichev, a Hasidic rabbi who lived in Russia during the early part of the nineteenth century. Levi Yitzhak was a man whose heart overflowed with love for the Jewish people. He was not afraid to rebuke God for allowing suffering and persecution to befall them. On one occasion, he compared the Jewish people to a pair of tefillin.

"Lord of the World," said Levi Yitzhak, "the people Israel are Your tefillin. When a simple Jew drops his tefillin, what does he do? He carefully picks them up. He cleans them. He kisses them, and restores them to their proper place. Lord of the World, I, Levi Yitzhak of Berdichev, have come to tell You. You have dropped Your tefillin."

Levi Yitzhak was not afraid to argue with God, but he would never condemn a Jewish person, even when he saw someone doing something obviously wrong.

On one such occasion, while walking down the street after the morning service, he came upon a teamster greasing the wheels of his wagon while still dressed in *tallit* and tefillin. Instead of scolding the man for soiling holy objects, he raised his eyes toward heaven and said aloud, "Lord of the World, look at this fellow! Look how devoted Your people Israel are! Even when greasing the wheels of a wagon, they still remember to praise Your Name!"

That is the purpose of *tallit* and tefillin: to remind us that every day, even in the midst of the most mundane chores, we must strive to live up to the highest ideals of the Jewish religion, to do our best to be a holy people, devoted to the service of God and to the welfare of our fellow human beings.

INTERVIEW ··

The only story I have to tell about my bar mitzvah actually took place two months before I went up to say my haftarah. One Sunday, I was supposed to go with my Uncle Butch to get my tallit and tefillin. Uncle Butch wasn't really my uncle. He was one of my father's best friends. I had known him all my life. Uncle Butch was very religious. He didn't have any children of his own, so it meant a lot to him to be the one to buy me my tallit and tefillin.

The night before we were supposed to go, my grandma asked me if I wanted to have my grandfather's tefillin. I was surprised that she still had them. My grandfather died in 1943, three years before I was born.

My grandma said she had been saving the tefillin for me all these years and that I could have them if I wanted them. She took them out of her closet and showed them to me. Most of my friends had little, tiny tefillin, about the size of matchbooks. These were huge! They were about three inches square, and you could tell by looking at them that they had seen a lot of use. Grandma told me a little about their history. They were made in Galicia close to a hundred years ago. Grandpa had received them on his bar mitzvah. He took them with him during his service in the Austrian army. He carried them across the ocean to America. He wore them from the time of his bar mitzvah to the day he died. And now they were mine.

However, they would have to be overhauled before I could wear them. The straps were so old and cracked they would fall apart if you tried to tighten them. The parchments inside the leather boxes might also have decayed over the years. A scribe would have to check them, and replace them if necessary.

When Uncle Butch came over on Sunday, I showed him the tefillin and asked if he knew any place I could bring them to have them repaired. Uncle Butch said he knew just the place.

We drove across Brooklyn to Williamsburg, where there are a lot of Hasidim. Uncle Butch and I climbed up three flights of stairs to a dusty little store that sold religious articles, prayer books, used Torah scrolls, Jewish antiques—you name it! The old man behind the counter asked us in Yiddish what we wanted. Uncle Butch said I needed a tallit for my bar mitzvah. He helped me pick out a really fine woolen one with black stripes. Then he told me to show the man my tefillin and explained to him that I wanted to know if they could be made usable.

The old man got really excited when he saw my tefillin. "These are old, really old," he said. Then he got down to business. "The straps are rotten. You'll need new ones."

"What about the parchments?" Uncle Butch asked.

"I can't tell till I open them up. If the parchments are no good, I'll give you new ones. I'll examine the boxes too. If there's any rot or damage, I can replace them."

"Just a minute," said Uncle Butch. "If you have new straps, new parchments, and new boxes, how is that different from new tefillin?"

It took the old man a few seconds to catch on. Then he started to laugh. "You're right. I got carried away. These boxes look like they're still in good shape. I think a new coat of paint is all they need. Come back next week and I'll have them ready."

So the next week, we went back and there were my tefillin, looking better than new. They had new straps and a new coat of lacquer.

"The parchments were fine," the man said. "I wish you could have seen them. Gorgeous writing. The scribes really knew their jobs back in those days. Here you are, sonny. A beautiful pair of new-old tefillin. Wear them well."

I did. I still do.

Eric A. Kimmel
Bar Mitzvah, 1959

TODAY I AM A MAN

··

An invitation to a
bar mitzvah ceremony

One who studies Torah as a child, to what can he be compared? To

ink written on fresh paper.

> *Rabbi Elisha ben Abuyah*
> The Sayings of the Fathers, *second century,* C.E.

What is it like to become bar mitzvah? An old story expresses it well.

In 1812, the French Emperor Napoleon invaded Russia. He defeated the Russians at the Battle of Borodino and occupied Moscow, where he planned to spend the winter. However, the city caught fire and burned to the ground almost immediately after the French marched in. Caught without sufficient food or shelter for his soldiers, Napoleon had no choice but to retreat. Bitter cold, disease, starvation, and constant attacks by peasant and Cossack guerrilla bands decimated his army. Napoleon's retreat from Moscow has gone down as one of the greatest disasters of military history.

The story goes that, during the retreat from Moscow, a sudden Cossack raid cut the emperor off from his troops. Napoleon escaped into the forest with the Cossacks hot on his heels. He ran until he was out of breath. Then, as if by a miracle, he saw an inn a short distance ahead. Summoning up his last strength, Napoleon ran to the inn. He pounded frantically on the door.

"Let me in! The Cossacks are after me!"

The innkeeper was a Jew named Mendel. He opened the door and, to his great surprise, saw the French emperor standing on the threshold.

"Save me! Hide me from the Cossacks!" Napoleon begged.

Mendel did not have much love for the French who had invaded his country. However, he was a kindly man who would never turn away someone in trouble.

"I will help you," Mendel said. "There's a haystack standing behind the stable. Hide yourself in the haystack. If the Cossacks ask, I will pretend I never saw you. With God's help, we will both survive."

Napoleon ran around the stable and buried himself deep inside the haystack. A few minutes later, a band of Cossacks rode up to the inn.

"Did you see a Frenchman run by here?"

"No," Mendel answered.

"You can't trust a Jew," the Cossack leader said. "Search the inn.

Search everywhere. The Frenchman couldn't have gotten away. He must be here someplace."

The Cossacks tore the inn apart. They turned over the beds and tables. They opened the cupboards and pulled out the linen, but they found no trace of Napoleon.

"He could be hiding in the stable," one of the Cossacks suggested. They searched the stable, the barn, the henhouse, and found nothing. They even thrust their lances deep into the haystack to make sure no one was hiding inside.

"He's not here," the Cossacks decided at last and rode off.

Only then did Napoleon emerge from the haystack. He trembled, for he had escaped death by inches. The lances had grazed his uniform three times and one had missed his head by the width of a finger.

Mendel took Napoleon into the inn and gave him a glass of brandy to restore his spirits. Soon afterward a troop of French cavalrymen rode up. The emperor was saved.

"I owe my life to you," Napoleon said as he kissed Mendel on both cheeks. "You deserve a reward. Ask for whatever you like and I, Napoleon, Emperor of France, will make sure you get it."

"I don't really need anything," Mendel replied, "but if you insist, I could use some help in putting my inn back together. And I would also like to ask you a question."

"What is it?"

"I would like to know what it felt like to be lying in that haystack while the Cossacks thrust their lances through it looking for you."

Napoleon's eyes blazed with anger. "How dare you ask the emperor of France a question like that!" He turned to his soldiers. "Tie this man to a tree and shoot him."

The soldiers obeyed the order at once. They tied Mendel to a tree, loaded their muskets, and formed a firing squad.

"Ready!" the captain said.

"Have mercy! Spare my life!" Mendel cried.

"Aim!" The soldiers pointed their weapons.

"*Shema Yisrael* . . ." The terrified innkeeper started murmuring the *Shema*, the prayer that Jews say before death.

The captain was about to give the command to fire, when Napoleon said, "Stop!" He ordered the soldiers to untie Mendel and let him go. As the soldiers lowered their rifles, the captain cut the ropes tying Mendel to the tree. The innkeeper collapsed in a dead faint.

After the soldiers revived Mendel, Napoleon said to him, "You wanted to know what it felt like to hide from the Cossacks in the haystack. Now you know."

Anyone who has ever prepared for a bar mitzvah celebration can identify with Napoleon and Mendel. What does it feel like to become bar mitzvah? It feels like you are king of the world. It also feels like you are about to be shot.

Preparing for Bar Mitzvah

The good news is that, over countless generations, every Jewish boy who has become bar mitzvah has felt the same way, and nearly all have survived the experience! It is also true that most boys preparing to become bar mitzvah don't start from ground zero. By regularly coming to synagogue on the Sabbath, they have learned about the different parts of the service and the Torah ritual. Through attendance at a Jewish day school or after-school religious classes, they have acquired at least a basic understanding of how the Hebrew language works and can read it with some degree of fluency. One of the biggest challenges is learning the haftarah.

The quickest and easiest way to learn a haftarah, though hardly the most rewarding, is to learn the words and melody by heart, just like learning a song in a foreign language. After all, no one needs to speak fluent French to sing *"Frère Jacques."* Cassette recordings of all the Torah and haftarah readings and the blessings that go with them are available for home study. And, sad to say, there are bar mitzvah ceremonies where the boy just rattles through his haftarah with no more idea of what he is saying than a parrot squawking, "Polly want a cracker!"

Most bar mitzvah classes offered through synagogues, day schools, and Hebrew schools provide far more than that. A competent teacher will make sure that a boy preparing for the ceremony understands, first of all, what becoming bar mitzvah means. He or she will talk about the basic beliefs and values of Judaism, as well as the responsibilities that a Jewish adult ought to fulfill. Instruction will begin by first reading the *parashah* of the week in English and thoroughly discussing it. Admittedly, some *parshiyot* are more interesting than others. Most people would rather read about the Garden of Eden, Noah's Ark, the Binding of Isaac, or the Exodus from Egypt than about complex rules governing sacrifices that haven't been offered in two thousand years. Nonetheless, each *parashah* is significant, and it is the teacher's responsibility to explain why.

The next step is to examine the haftarah, discussing how it is related to the *parashah* and why it is important in its own right. The teacher will have the student read through the haftarah in Hebrew, making sure he understands the vocabulary and is pronouncing the words correctly. Once the student becomes familiar with the Hebrew text, the teacher will begin instructing him in the chant. Since learning the chant is largely a matter of repetition and practice, the teacher may record the haftarah or provide a commercial recording so the student can study at home.

If the student is willing to devote additional time to preparation, the teacher may show him how the musical notation system works. Once the student has mastered that, he can read any haftarah or Torah portion. It is not unusual to find an especially gifted or devoted student acting as *baal korei* at his own bar mitzvah, reading the Torah as well as the haftarah.

Imagine what it would be like to become bar mitzvah.

The Day Arrives

You hardly sleep the night before. You lie awake, going over the blessings and the readings again and again in your mind. You think of all sorts of terrible things that might happen: *What if I forget the haftarah right in the middle? What if I get so nervous I throw up on the Torah? Has that ever happened? Would God forgive me? Has anyone ever died from becoming bar mitzvah?*

In the morning, you get dressed and put on your new suit. You sit down to have breakfast with your family, but you don't feel like eating. Your mother encourages you to have something, pointing out that it is going to be a long day. You know she's right. You try, but every mouthful seems to stick in your throat. You wish you were a million miles away, on another planet, or even another galaxy. A year ago, when you began your bar mitzvah studies, it seemed that this day would never arrive. Now it is here, having come so fast you are still not certain that it is really happening.

If your family is Orthodox, you will walk to the synagogue together. If not, and you live some distance away, you will probably ride. You keep hoping that the car won't get lost on the way, and at the same time, you hope it will.

People are already gathering at the synagogue. They look up and smile when you arrive. Several seats have been reserved for you and your family at the front of the synagogue. You put on your *tallit* and are pleased to find that your mind hasn't gone completely blank. You still remember the blessing. As you take your seat, you notice the rabbi and the cantor watching you from their places on the *bimah*. They nod to you and you nod back, surprised that they appear to be so confident when you're so nervous. Your bar mitzvah teacher comes over to say hello. He will be acting as *baal korei* today. You're glad to have a friend on the *bimah* with you—just in case.

"Today's the big day. How do you feel?" he asks.

"Fine," you answer. Your voice comes out in a scared little squeak.

"Don't worry. You'll do a great job," your teacher tells you. He winks at your father. "I haven't lost one yet." Your father chuckles. Is he remembering his own bar mitzvah celebration?

Your mother whispers, "Don't worry about a thing. You're going to do just fine." How can she be so sure? She never had a bar mitzvah celebration. You wonder if she really believes that, or if she's just saying it because she's your mom.

The seats fill up as more people arrive—young, old, and everything in between. You see some of your friends from school. They all sit together in the back. The girls wave and giggle. You've never seen them so dressed up before. They really look good, like they were going to a high school prom! The guys give you high fives and thumbs up signs, as if this were a basketball game. They're a little boisterous, but no one seems to mind. It seems strange to see your friends who aren't Jewish wearing kippot. You must look even stranger to them in your *tallit*! Just the same, you're glad they're here. They may not know what's going on; they may never have been in a synagogue before, but you know they're behind you all the way.

A baby starts crying. Two little kids chase each other up and down the aisles until the usher escorts them back to their parents. People come up to congratulate you. Their faces go by in a blur. Some are relatives, some are old family friends, and some you're sure you've never seen before. But they all know you—usually from the time you were a baby. Your great-aunt leans over to pinch your cheek. "Such a lovely boy!" she says, loud enough for the whole congregation to hear. "I still remember the first time I held you in my lap and you wet your diaper."

You feel like sinking into the floor with embarrassment.

"Shhh!" several people say.

Jewish services often get rambunctious. The decorum of a cathedral is definitely not part of the tradition. However, everyone settles down as soon as the cantor begins the *Borchu* prayer, signifying the start of the main part of the service. You stand and bow, sit and stand with the rest of the congregation. The ancient Hebrew melodies take hold and carry you along, like a boat drifting downstream. You don't feel as nervous as you did before.

Then suddenly, before you realize it, you find yourself heading for a waterfall. The prayers that used to take so long to get through seem to have gone by at supersonic speed. The ark is open. The Torah service is about to begin.

The Torah is taken out of the ark. Your teacher leads the procession, carrying the scroll you are going to read from. He stops in front of you. You raise the corner of your *tallit,* press it against one of the embroidered lions on the mantle, and bring it to your lips.

Before you realize it, the scroll has been unwrapped and laid out on the reader's desk. The *baal korei* calls the first *aliyah.* Your father's friend from the office is a *Kohen.* He looks pleased to accept the honor. He says the blessing in a strong clear voice. The *baal korei* begins reading the *parashah.* He seems to be going much too fast because now the second *aliyah* is being called. This is the husband of one of your mother's friends, who is a *Levi.* It's clear he probably hasn't said these blessings since his own bar mitzvah ceremony. The *baal korei* has to remind him to kiss the Torah with his *tallit.* He stumbles over the words and loses his place, but manages to get through with a little help. *I can do better than that,* you think to yourself. Suddenly you start feeling more confident.

The third *aliyah* goes to your father. He has been practicing every day for two weeks to make sure he does it right. He brings it off without a hitch. He looks to you and you give him the high sign.

The next four *aliyot* go by as if they were on rollerblades, and the next thing you know the *baal korei* is chanting the words you have been waiting for. He calls you by your Hebrew name to come up to receive the *maftir aliyah*.

"That's you!" your brother whispers, as if you didn't know your own name. This is it! You want to get up, but you're frozen in your seat. Your brother gives you a shove. Somehow you make it to your feet. Your mother squeezes your hand as you go by. "You'll be great," she says. She sounds so convinced that you almost believe it yourself.

You get to the *bimah,* but you're so nervous you go up the stairs to the right instead of the ones to the left. You're already halfway up by the time you realize it. It's too late to turn around and go back, so you just keep on going.

The traffic jam at the top of the stairs gets sorted out. You find yourself standing where you belong, next to your teacher. "Think you can handle it?" he whispers.

"I know I can," you say.

"Go for it." He takes the *yad* and points to the word that begins the next section. You're not afraid or nervous. You know what to do. Taking the corner of your *tallit,* you press the *tzitzit* against the parchment and kiss it. Then you place your hands on the handles of the scroll and say the blessings.

As you stand on the *bimah* looking out over the congregation, it occurs to you that just about everyone you ever knew in your life is there: your parents, your brothers and sisters, your friends, relatives, and neighbors. Everyone has come to be with you on this day. The *baal korei* hands you the *yad*. You grasp it firmly and begin reading the *maftir*'s portion. The ancient letters flicker like sparks of black fire as the miniature hand moves across the parchment.

"The Letters Fly up to Heaven"

In the back of your mind, you recall a story your teacher told you when you first began learning how to read this portion. When the Romans condemned Rabbi Hananiah to be burned alive for teaching the Torah, they tied him to a stake and wound Torah scrolls around his body. As the scrolls began to burn, Rabbi Hananiah's students called out to him, "Rabbi, what do you see?" He answered, "I see the parchment burning, but the letters . . . the letters fly up to heaven!"

Now you understand what that story means. Suddenly you are aware that there are other people standing with you. You cannot see them, but you feel their presence—aged rabbis bent over yellowing pages of Talmud; old women lighting Sabbath candles; a family standing together on the edge of a corpse-filled pit, looking not at the bodies below, but at the sky above; young pioneers, men and women, building a new nation in an ancient land with hands on the plow and rifles on their shoulders. They are all here—people of the book and people of the sword; dwellers in tents and dwellers in palaces, those who spoke with peasants and those who conversed with kings.

Now you understand what it means to become bar mitzvah. You are part of them, as they are a part of you. For they are the Jewish people, your ancestors, going back to the time of Abraham, the first human being to surrender himself to God.

Words from the Heart

The rest passes like a dream. You chant the haftarah, and the words flow effortlessly, as if you were singing a favorite song.

Now comes the time for your *Dvar Torah*. You take the speech from your pocket, unfold it, and place it on the lectern, as you have seen the rabbi do each Saturday. Everybody looks up at you, as if expecting words of wisdom. You're not sure that what you have to say is wise, but it is sincere. When you first began preparing this speech, your teacher said, "Don't try to be a Talmud scholar. Be yourself. You know what the *parashah* and the haftarah are saying. Write about what that message means to you."

And so you talk about what you know—how some people your age wear two-hundred-dollar sneakers and others sleep in the park; how a friend of yours carries a loaded pistol to school, not because he wants to hurt anybody, but because he's afraid to walk down the street without it. You recall a girl in your class who tried to end her life before it had even begun. Perhaps some adults don't think thirteen-year-olds should know about these things. But you do.

And then you talk about the *parashah* and the haftarah, and what these ancient words mean to you. There is no applause when you finish. There never is, in a synagogue. You're not sure that everybody understood what you were trying to say. You know you didn't solve all the world's problems. But you meant every word. According to your teacher, that's what really matters.

Then, before you realize it, it is over. The Torah is returned to the ark and you return to your seat, shaking hands and accepting congratulations all the way. You feel happy, but exhausted, as if you've just run a marathon.

To Life!

After the service is over, your family hosts a reception, a *Kiddush*. There is hallah, wine, and cake. Everyone waits while you recite the blessings; first over wine, then over bread. "*L'chayim!*" they all say as they drink. It is a traditional Jewish toast that means, "To life!"

Now you're beginning to get hungry, but you don't have time to eat because it seems that everyone wants to talk to you at once. You're hugged and kissed and patted on the back. Your parents almost have to drag you out of the synagogue so you'll have time to rest before the party.

More than a year ago, when your parents first began planning your bar mitzvah party, they agreed on certain conditions. They wanted an informal affair, so everyone could feel at home and have a good time. The party would take place in the evening, after the Sabbath, so that your observant friends and relatives would be able to attend. The food would be strictly kosher. You and your parents had a long discussion about this. The three of you decided that while your family might be less than fully observant of the dietary rules in your daily lives, an affair honoring your entry in Jewish adulthood should not openly violate Jewish law. Your parents made out a budget and stuck to it. Your bar mitzvah celebration might not be as elaborate as others, but you felt relieved knowing your parents weren't going to have to mortgage your home to pay for a party.

And what a party! You've waited all year for this. Tonight's your night. You're the star! And you feel like one, too, especially when the photographer's flash goes off in your face every ten seconds. Your parents warned you to expect this. Everybody wants to have a picture taken with the bar mitzvah boy.

Your aunt is in charge of the presents. The big boxes are being kept in another room. However, people keep coming up to you, handing you envelopes. Your pockets are bulging with them. "This is for college," they say as if they are kidding, but they're not. Gifts of money are traditional at a bar mitzvah celebration, and more than one college education has been partially financed with such gifts.

You have also received several books. This is to be expected, since books are a traditional bar mitzvah gift, especially books on Jewish subjects. So far you have received a Bible, a history of the Jewish people, a three-volume collection of folktales and legends, and a lavishly illustrated book about famous Jews in sports. There's even a book about becoming bar mitzvah!

And people keep handing you pens. Everyone treats this as a joke, and it is. In the early years of this century, the fountain pen was a new invention, and giving a pen as a gift quickly became a tradition. With the pen came the hope that the recipient would devote himself to his studies, graduate from high school, then college, and make a career as a professional: one who works with his brain instead of his muscles. You can be sure people are joking when they stick a cheap ballpoint in your pocket. But there's no joke about what the pen symbolizes. It represents a sincere wish that you will grow up to be an educated person with a lifelong love and respect for books and learning.

Now it's time to eat. You can't have a Jewish celebration without great food—lots of it! The buffet table almost sags in the middle. There's corned beef, pastrami, tongue, derma, kugel, kasha, turkey, a gigantic hallah and thick loaves of pumpernickel and rye bread, as well as a host of other Jewish delicacies you've never tasted before. In spite of temptation, you don't dare eat too much because you have to save room for dessert—a mouth-watering spread of cakes, pies, and traditional Jewish treats like rugelach and halvah.

Music is as important as food. There's a DJ spinning records to get everybody warmed up. Every one is a favorite, because you picked them all. After a few minutes, it's obvious your older relatives don't share your taste in music, but who cares? It's your party. And in a little while there's going to be a treat that everyone will enjoy.

Jewish Jazz

It's a klezmer band—the Klezmeshuginers—playing songs and dances of Eastern Europe that your great-grandparents knew. It's the wildest collection of musicians and instruments you've ever seen. There's an accordion, drums, a big double bass, two violins, and a banjo. The real show is the clarinetist. His name is Jamal, he's African American, and he wears his hair in long dreadlocks with a green, black, and red kippah pinned on top. And can he play! The clarinet soars and wails. You never knew such sounds could come out of an instrument.

"For those of you who are thinking, 'Funny, this guy doesn't look Jewish,'" Mr. Jamal explains during a break, "I got interested in klezmer music when I was studying clarinet at the Juilliard School of Music in New York. Klezmer, you know, is Jewish jazz. So it just comes naturally to this boy from the Motor City, who's gonna cut loose now with a classic klezmer song by that great composer, Aaron Lebedeff. When we come to the chorus, you yell 'Zetz!' as loud as you can. That means 'Gimme a beat!' Here we go. One . . . two . . . " He lifts his clarinet and leads the band into a blistering rendition of Lebedeff's "Romania." At the chorus, everyone yells "Zetz!" and stamps so hard the dishes on the table jump.

The last dance is a hora. You, your parents, your brothers and sisters, your friends from school, form a big circle in the middle of the room. The steps are easy enough for anyone to learn in a

minute. The music starts slowly, then picks up speed until you are whirling around faster and faster. The circle grows larger as more and more people join in. When it gets so big it can't expand anymore, it breaks into a long line that snakes in and out among the tables.

"Havah nagilah, havah nagilah, v'nismecha . . ."

You dance until you're out of breath and so tired you can hardly put one foot ahead of another. And still, you don't want it to end.

The party is nearly over. You look toward your parents, and you're surprised to see your mother dabbing at her eyes with her handkerchief. You wonder why she's crying. You've never been happier in your life.

• BAR MITZVAH •

An End, and a Beginning

In the car on the way home, you think about your bar mitzvah day. On the one hand, you're glad it's finally over and that life can return to normal. Music, sports, hanging out with your friends, and so many other things you enjoy have all had to take a back seat this past year while you prepared for your bar mitzvah ceremony. At the same time, you feel a touch of sadness that something that has been such an important part of your life for so long has ended. Most important, you feel proud of yourself. You know you did well today. You also learned something about yourself: that you have the drive and the discipline to achieve any goal.

Just before you fall asleep, your parents come into your room to say good night. "You were wonderful today," your mother says. "I always knew you would be."

"What made you so sure?" you ask.

"Mothers can always tell," she answers.

Your father sits down on the edge of your bed. He says, "I remember when I had my bar mitzvah celebration. After it was over I thought, *I wonder what it will be like to see my son become bar mitzvah*. Now I know."

"I was thinking the same thing," you tell him.

"I hope we'll all be there to see it," your mother says.

"So do I," you say, and close your eyes. You fall asleep, wondering about the future and what it will bring.

But no matter what lies ahead, as long as there are Jewish parents and Jewish sons, there will always be bar mitzvah celebrations.

INTERVIEW ···

My bar mitzvah was disappointing because I never got a chance to say my haftarah. Don't think I didn't know how. I had a fine Jewish education. I can read all the haftarot *as easily as I can read the newspaper.*

What happened is that my bar mitzvah celebration fell on a special Sabbath. It's called Shabbat Shuvah, *which means "the Sabbath of Repentance." It's the Saturday between Rosh Hashanah and Yom Kippur. Shabbat Shuvah is one of the most important Sabbaths of the year, coming as it does before Yom Kippur. Now on this particular Sabbath, there was another boy besides myself having his bar mitzvah. And he was a* Kohen, *which meant that he took precedence. So he got to say the haftarah and I just had an* aliyah.

That bothered me; not having had the chance to read the haftarah on my own bar mitzvah, especially when I knew I could do it. I always felt that somehow my bar mitzvah wasn't complete. I could have asked to be maftir *the next year, or the year after that. The problem was Shabbat Shuvah. It was such an important Sabbath that if there wasn't a bar mitzvah celebration going on, the honor of* maftir *went to one of the sages in our synagogue, one of the really learned old men with the long beards. A kid like me never had a chance for a* maftir *on that day.*

Years went by, and I still hadn't said my haftarah.

Then one year, I was visiting my son and his family in New Jersey. I was eighty years old and retired by then. It was the week before Shabbat Shuvah, so I naturally started thinking about my bar mitzvah. I asked myself, how much longer are you going to wait? If you don't say that haftarah now, who knows if you'll get another chance? After all, when you're eighty years old, you can't automatically assume you're going to be around for another year. So I asked my son to talk to his rabbi and find out if the maftir *for Shabbat Shuvah was available. If it was, I would like to have it.*

After my son explained the situation, the rabbi called me up and personally invited me to take the maftir. *He thought it was a terrific idea that I would finally be able to complete my bar mitzvah after sixty-seven years.*

You'd think I'd be nervous as Saturday approached, but I wasn't. Like I said, I know all the haftarot. *It was my son who got nervous. I told him not to worry. I was going to read that haftarah through without making one mistake.*

And I did. Leave it to an eighty-year-old man to show those bar mitzvah boys how it's done. My son was so proud, he threw his arms around me and gave me a big hug in front of everybody. And that's not all. Guess what he did after I finished? He gave me a fountain pen! Not an ordinary fountain pen either, but an antique Waterman—just the kind I would have gotten at my bar mitzvah sixty-seven years before.

Ralph Podell
Bar Mitzvah, 1920

IF NOT NOW, WHEN?

....

An ancient ceremony meets
the modern age

Where does God dwell? Wherever people let him in.

Rabbi Menahem Mendel of Kotsk
Poland, nineteenth century

The story is told that when Rabbi Mordecai of Lekhovitz died, his son, Rabbi Noah, succeeded him. Rabbi Noah had the reputation of being an innovator. He liked to change things, if for no other reason than to shake people out of their old habits.

Some of the old rabbi's followers worried that Rabbi Noah would turn everything upside down. They came to him and nervously asked, "Are you planning to make any changes, now that you have taken your father's place?"

Rabbi Noah reassured them. "Don't worry. I'm going to do exactly what my father did."

At the next Sabbath service, Rabbi Noah turned everything not only upside down, but inside out. When his father used to stand up, he sat. And when his father sat, he stood up. When his father prayed silently, he called out the words in his loudest voice. And where his father used to speak in a loud voice, he whispered. Nothing was the way it used to be.

After the service, Rabbi Mordecai's followers came to Rabbi Noah and said, "You are the rabbi and we must accept whatever you do. However, we cannot understand why you would lie to us."

"When did I lie to you?" Rabbi Noah asked, genuinely surprised.

"Don't you remember? We came to you and asked if you planned to make any changes in the way your father did things. You assured us you would do exactly as your father did. Then you went and turned everything on its head. Nothing is the way it was in your father's time."

Rabbi Noah answered, "My friends, I am sorry you misunderstood me. When I said I was going to do exactly as my father did, I didn't mean I was going to keep everything the way it was. When my father took over from his father sixty years ago, he made many important changes. That is what I meant when I said I was going to do exactly what my father did. He never copied anyone and neither will I. In that way, I will be doing exactly what my father did."

Traditions New and Old

Throughout history, Jewish customs and practices have evolved to meet new challenges and conditions. Many age-old traditions, when closely examined, turn out to be neither as old nor as traditional as is commonly assumed.

For example, the Jewish custom of covering one's head with a hat or *kippah* during worship is not mentioned in the Torah and there is only one reference to it in the Talmud. People bringing sacrifices to the Temple in Jerusalem most likely came before the altar bareheaded. Even as late as the thirteenth century, the practice of covering the head was not universally observed, even by those being called up to the Torah.

Another distinctly Jewish custom is to have the groom crush a glass underfoot at the wedding ceremony. The explanation usually given for this practice is that this serves as a reminder of the destruction of the Temple. However, another possible reason for breaking the glass has nothing to do with the Temple. The custom may have begun during the time of the Talmud, when two rabbis smashed expensive glassware at their sons' weddings to prevent the drinking and revelry from getting out of hand.

Finally, the best-known and most frequently observed Jewish holiday in the United States today is neither Rosh Hashanah nor Yom Kippur, but Hanukkah, a holiday that is not mentioned in the Bible and that was never more than a minor festival. Why the change? There are two reasons. The first is obvious—Hanukkah comes at the same time as Christmas. It gives Jewish children an opportunity to receive gifts and enjoy the holiday season without having to take part in a Christian celebration. But there is another reason as well. Hanukkah started to become more important at the end of the nineteenth century. This period, which also marks the beginning of the Zionist movement, was a time of savage anti-Semitic persecution and great political unrest. The Hanukkah celebration recalled an age when Jews were not helpless victims, but heroic fighters who stood with swords in hand in one of the world's first fights for religious freedom.

Customs Change

Lavish bar mitzvah celebrations are another one of those "age-old" traditions that are neither as age-old nor as traditional as people like to think. Until about seventy years ago, most bar mitzvah celebrations tended to be modest affairs. The boy received an *aliyah,* but frequently did not recite a haftarah. The bar mitzvah ceremony might not even be held on the Sabbath. Many bar mitzvah ceremonies took place at the Monday or Thursday morning service. Asked to describe their own bar mitzvah experiences, the great-grandfathers of today's boys usually shrug and say, "They called me up for an *aliyah.* I said the blessings. My father put a bottle of schnapps on the table. Everybody drank *l'chaim,* and that was it."

A Struggle to Survive

There are several reasons for the vast difference between the way becoming bar mitzvah was celebrated during the first decades of this century and the way it is celebrated today.

116

One reason is economic. At the beginning of the twentieth century, most Jewish families in Europe and America were desperately poor. In Russia, where the ancestors of many American Jews came from, conditions were especially bad. Providing food and shelter for one's family was a daily struggle. People lived on a constant diet of black bread, potatoes, and herring, and considered themselves lucky to get it.

Conditions in America were far better than they were in Europe. If nothing else, American Jews did not have to contend with governments that made anti-Semitism an official policy. Nonetheless, from 1880 to 1920, the survival of many Jewish immigrant families depended on child labor. Children worked before, after, and often during the hours when they were supposed to be attending school. Frequently, even that wasn't enough. The famous composer Irving Berlin had to leave home one year after his bar mitzvah celebration. His father had died and his mother could no longer afford to feed him.

It is easy to see why bar mitzvah celebrations of the time were modest. Few families could afford to host a large affair.

Lack of money, however, is not the only reason. Jewish families of the time had different priorities. Providing educations for their sons and respectable weddings and doweries for their daughters was seen as far more important than celebrating a bar mitzvah.

By the late 1930s, conditions and outlooks started to change. The American Jewish community began to prosper, and with prosperity came the desire to make up for the deprivations of the past. Dr. Cohen's father may have sold bananas from a pushcart. His own bar mitzvah ceremony may have been a Monday morning *aliyah,* a bottle of home-brewed cherry brandy, and a few pieces of cake. However, Dr. Cohen's son would recite the whole haftarah. His bar mitzvah celebration would be on Saturday, with a lavish reception to which two hundred people would be invited. In this way, Dr. Cohen could show his friends, his relatives, his neighbors, his professional colleagues, and the whole world that the Cohen family had arrived!

Priorities changed as well. In Eastern Europe, Jews had a distinct culture with its own language, customs, and traditions. They had little to do with their non-Jewish neighbors. Most Polish and Russian Jews could neither read nor speak the language of the country. In America, however, this was not the case. One could be Jewish and still participate in American culture. American Jewish boys and girls attended public schools. They spoke English. They played sports and followed contemporary fashions. Jewish parents saw their children turning into Americans and wondered if this might not be too much of a good thing. Would their children remain Jewish?

Making a Commitment

The bar mitzvah celebration began to grow in importance in response to this concern. Preparing for a bar mitzvah ceremony required a Jewish education. It required a boy to think seriously about his religious and cultural identity. It reaffirmed the link between the past and the future.

For these reasons, most modern bar mitzvah celebrations are marked in a way that would have been possible for only the wealthiest families a century ago. They are held on Saturday so that the boy can take part in the Sabbath service. He is expected to be able to recite the haftarah. Usually, there is a *kiddush* at the synagogue at the conclusion of the service, and a larger reception or party afterward.

Bat Mitzvah

The elevation of the bar mitzvah ceremony from minor to major event is not the only innovation to occur in America. Even more revolutionary is the idea of a bar mitzvah ceremony for girls—the "bat mitzvah."

The bat mitzvah celebration is an entirely American invention. At the beginning of the century, women had no role in the traditional synagogue service. The synagogue was a man's world. Women were welcome as long as they knew their place, which was either up in the women's gallery or on the other side of a divider several feet high. Women could kiss the Torah as it came by, but the idea of a woman being called up for an *aliyah* or a woman *maftir* reading the haftarah was unacceptable.

Orthodox congregations still separate men and women during religious services, as has been the custom in synagogues for centuries. Reform, Conservative, and other groups allow mixed seating. People who are offended by the idea of segregated seating are not likely to be convinced by any of the explanations offered in its defense, but they should not automatically assume that Judaism is a sexist religion that downgrades women.

Judaism has always held women in high esteem, but sees men and women as having different areas of responsibility. In the ideal

Jewish household, the wife was responsible for managing the home and supervising family life while the husband occupied himself with earning a living, prayer, and study. *The Memoirs of Glueckel of Hameln* (1645–1724) presents a fascinating portrait of a dynamic Jewish woman who exemplified this ideal. Glueckel was not only a devoted wife and the loving mother of twelve children, but a shrewd businesswoman who advised her husband in all his enterprises and carried on his business after his death.

A woman with small children to watch and a meal cooking on the stove could not be expected to drop everything and run off to the synagogue for morning and afternoon prayers. Consequently, the Rabbis exempted women from *mitzvot* that have to be performed at specific times of the day. The synagogue thus became men's domain. Men were required to be there. Women were not.

However, times and customs change. What was accepted in the past without question was increasingly challenged. By 1940, the first generation of American-born Jewish women of Eastern European descent was not content to stay home to cook, clean, and look after children. Unlike their mothers and grandmothers, these women had received some formal education. They challenged the notion that women had no part in the synagogue service. They demanded to have families sit together, as they did in Reform synagogues and Christian churches: mothers and daughters sitting with fathers and sons.

The idea of bar mitzvah celebrations as a male monopoly also came under fire, especially since it had now become a much more important event. Why all this attention and expense for boys and nothing for girls? Can't a girl learn a haftarah? Can't a girl take an active role in the service? Can't a girl benefit from a first-rate Jewish education?

There was no reason why girls could not, and every reason they should. If the experience of bar mitzvah deepened a boy's understanding and commitment to Judaism, shouldn't a girl have the same experience? The bat mitzvah ceremony arose out of this demand for equality and increased recognition for women. In 1922, twelve-year-old Judith Kaplan celebrated the first bat mitzvah. But it wasn't until the 1950s that bat mitzvah celebrations became a tradition among nearly all Jewish groups in the United States and abroad. The Orthodox are the exception, for they usually maintain the older tradition of calling only men to the Torah.

Adult Bar Mitzvah

Another new development is the growing number of older men choosing to become bar mitzvah if they had not done so as boys. A boy might not have had a bar mitzvah celebration for several reasons. Some families were too poor to afford even a meager celebration. Others were Socialists or Communists who did not believe in religion. Sometimes the family was willing, but the boy was not. Many older Jewish men will admit that they were tough street kids who wanted no part of an old-fashioned religion that got in the way of their becoming one-hundred-percent Americans. Other boys who grew up in Europe spent their thirteenth birthdays as refugees or as prisoners in concentration camps, where staying alive was a struggle. Needless to say, they had no opportunity to celebrate becoming bar mitzvah.

A computer search of newspapers around the country turns up some interesting stories.

- Coral Springs, Florida—Benny Rubin and his grandson Robert Lewis celebrated together. Mr. Rubin is seventy-four years old. He missed his bar mitzvah ceremony because he was thrown out of his Hebrew school class, the former boxer told *The Broward Jewish World*. "It's about time I started to be an adult," he said.

  What did Mr. Rubin's grandson think about sharing the bar mitzvah spotlight with his grandfather? "It's cool," said seventh-grader Robert Lewis.

- Beverly Hills, California—Jimmy Getzoff, a classical violinist and former concertmaster of the Glendale Symphony Orchestra, became bar mitzvah at Temple Emanuel, to celebrate his seventieth birthday. He began preparing for the ceremony five months ago, working with a rabbi and a private tutor. He studied three to four hours every day.

  "It just came to me that I wanted to do something exceptional for my next birthday," Mr. Getzoff told the *Los Angeles Times*. "I needed this now more than any other time in my life. This experience has given me a sense of who I am and what it really means to be Jewish. It's the beginning and not the end. I will continue to go on learning."

- Graterford, Pennsylvania—Bennett Seidman, forty-one years old, celebrated becoming bar mitzvah at Graterford State Prison, a maximum security institution forty miles northwest of Philadelphia, where he is serving a five-to-ten-year sentence. Mr. Seidman told a reporter from the *Los Angeles Times* that while he had been raised in a Jewish home, he had defied his parents by refusing to go through with his bar mitzvah ceremony. Now he says, "I always felt there was this void in my life. And I wanted to do this to make my parents proud of me."

Prison officials pointed out that Seidman is possibly the first inmate in the Pennsylvania prison system to have a bar mitzvah ceremony. The ceremony was performed in the only all-inmate synagogue within prison walls in the United States.

• Mission Viejo, California—Bernard Modelevsky, eighty-five years old, finally celebrated the bar mitzvah ceremony that was postponed for seventy-two years by the Russian Revolution.

Mr. Modelevsky grew up in an Orthodox Jewish home in the Russian town of Zhitomir. With the outbreak of the Russian Revolution, the country dissolved into chaos and civil war. Pogroms and persecution drove the Modelevskys from their home before Bernard could celebrate becoming bar mitzvah.

At his bar mitzvah ceremony at the Heritage Point Retirement Home, Mr. Modelevsky read from a Torah sent from his former synagogue in Minnesota. His father, his grandfather, and his sons have all read from that same scroll.

"When you're thirteen, that's the big day," Mr. Modelevsky said. "When you're eighty-five, you become thirteen again. It's a great honor. It's a wonderful dream. I lived for this."

Bar Mitzvahmania!

Becoming bar mitzvah has developed into a tremendously popular custom. Unfortunately, the desire to make the bar mitzvah celebration a special event sometimes overshadows what becoming bar mitzvah is really supposed to mean.

A bar mitzvah celebration is a religious occasion. It recognizes a Jewish boy's taking on the responsibilities of manhood and confirms his lifelong commitment to the Jewish religion and the Jewish people. Without that commitment, the bar mitzvah celebration has no meaning.

Yet many people treat the bar mitzvah celebration as just an excuse to hold a big party. Tens of thousands of dollars are spent on extravagant bashes that have nothing to do with the Jewish way of life, and what is worse, make a mockery of it. "Too much *bar* and not enough *mitzvah*," is a frequently heard complaint that describes such bacchanals.

It is easy to laugh at such outlandish displays as a life-size chopped liver statue of Moses holding the Ten Commandments, but even that seems quaint compared to what "bar mitzvah professionals" can come up with. A 1990 trade show in Los Angeles showed what a bar mitzvah celebration can be if good taste isn't allowed to get in the way. How about a giant cake shaped like a Torah? A video wall? The boy's name on a movie marquee? Do you like clowns, mimes? What about a clown parachuting into the middle of your bar mitzvah party? How about an elephant? How about a dozen, or a line of cheerleaders from the Los Angeles Lakers? You can have a man with a giant Elvis head, or smoke and lights and all kinds of theatrical effects. Would you like to see the boy arrive in a silver space ship? How's that for special!

"I want M.C. Hammer at my bar mitzvah ceremony," said one nine-year-old visitor. Michael Bernstone, age 12, was much less impressed. "This is weird," he said. Michael may have been the most perceptive person at the gathering.

If parachuting clowns, high-kicking cheerleaders, and Elvis impersonators appear to be the outer limits of bar mitzvahmania, consider the case of the "bar mitzvah belly dancer."

Ilana Raskin is a professional belly dancer, one of several who entertain at weddings and bar mitzvah celebrations throughout Israel. In fairness to Ms. Raskin, the idea of a belly dancer at a bar mitzvah celebration is not as bizarre as it seems. Hiring a dancer to entertain at festive events is a tradition among Sephardic Jews. According to Ms. Raskin, "Our costumes are not modest, but nor are they overly erotic. It is an accepted custom for many Israelis."

The Israeli rabbinate did not see it that way. Belly dancing is obscene, they argued. Rabbis authorized to certify that food served in restaurants and hotels is kosher began withdrawing certificates from places that allowed belly dancing.

This created a problem for the dancers. No Orthodox Jew will eat in a place where the food is not certified to be kosher, and many Israeli Jews are Orthodox. Bookings for belly dancers began drying up.

Ilana Raskin took the rabbis to court. She argued that the authority to certify that food was kosher did not give them the right to censor entertainment. The judges ruled in Ms. Raskin's favor.

Alternative Celebrations

Such high jinks aside, the vast majority of bar mitzvah celebrations are dignified events where everybody has a good time without losing sight of what a bar mitzvah ceremony is supposed to represent. However, a number of young people and their families are exploring new ways to celebrate and are coming up with exciting alternatives.

An increasing number of families are choosing to celebrate in Israel. The most popular sites are the Western Wall in Jerusalem and the Masada fortress overlooking the Dead Sea, where a band of Jewish patriots held off the Roman army. The Israeli Ministry of Tourism estimates that forty-five-hundred people from all over the world celebrated becoming a bar or bat mitzvah in Israel during 1993. Not all are teenagers. A growing number of adults come to Israel every year to celebrate becoming bar mitzvah, too.

It recently become possible to celebrate becoming a bar mitzvah on Ellis Island in New York Harbor. The reception center on Ellis Island was the gateway to America for tens of thousands of Jewish families. The buildings on Ellis Island stood in ruins for years. Recently renovated, they offer facilities for conferences and receptions—including bar mitzvah celebrations.

Helping Others

Hillel, a great teacher who lived during the time of the Second Temple, said, "If I am not for myself, who am I? If I am only for myself, what am I? If not now, when?" Many people believe becoming a bar mitzvah should include more than just a synagogue service and a reception. They feel it ought to reflect Hillel's words. Becoming a bar mitzvah should be an occasion for joy and celebration, but if it is only about *me* and how many gifts *I* receive, then it loses its meaning. Becoming bar mitzvah should be a time to think of others as well as oneself. More important, it should be a time to act.

An increasing number of boys and girls participating in bar and bat mitzvah classes across the country are making it a point to include a special project as part of their preparation. They volunteer to work in old-age homes, day-care centers, shelters for the homeless. Others raise money for causes ranging from local food banks to disaster relief and international aid projects around the world.

Mazon—the Hebrew word for "food"—is a Jewish aid project that raises funds to buy food for hungry people in the United States and other countries. It asks American Jews to support its efforts by donating three percent of the cost of wedding, bar mitzvah, and other celebrations. This is in keeping with the ancient Torah commandment to tithe ourselves to benefit the poor.

Adam Shapiro of Temple Beth Am in Abington, Pennsylvania, decided he wanted to do more. He took it upon himself to launch a children's campaign to benefit Mazon. Adam spoke to five bar and bat mitzvah classes at his temple. He told his friends about millions of starving people all over the world and what Mazon does to help them. He urged them to include a pledge to Mazon as part of their bar and bat mitzvah celebrations. Forty-eight of Adam's classmates volunteered to participate.

Sometimes such a project can launch a lifetime of work for worthy causes. Stanley Hirsch grew up in New York City during the Depression. His father worked in a gas station. When Stanley was preparing to become bar mitzvah, his rabbi asked him to collect money for the Jewish National Fund, to help build a Jewish homeland in what was then the British Mandate of Palestine.

Mr. Hirsch told a reporter for the *Los Angeles Times,* "I took one of these little blue cans and walked around in the Bronx. It was my first taste of going out and raising money—nickels and dimes and pennies. They just asked that you bring the box back full."

Fifty years and millions of dollars later, Mr. Hirsch is still collecting money for worthy causes. He and his wife Anita have raised funds to help Jews escape from Ethiopia, to resettle Soviet Jews in Israel, to establish the United States Holocaust Memorial Museum in Washington, D.C., to build a park and a community center for the people of Ajami, an Arab section of Tel Aviv.

The Meaning of Becoming Bar Mitzvah

What is the real reason for a bar mitzvah celebration? As was pointed out earlier, the phrase means, "one who has the obligation to fulfill the commandments." Within a few years, many Jewish boys who are becoming bar mitzvah today will be serving in the armies of their nations. In Israel, nearly all will. In many ways, becoming bar mitzvah is like a soldier volunteering to serve. Loyal soldiers may never meet their commanding general face-to-face, but by carrying out his orders they fulfill his will and express their devotion to him.

Some would say that orders are to be obeyed without question. One hundred years ago many people believed this. Soldiers were not supposed to think for themselves. They were to do exactly as they were told. "Theirs not to reason why/Theirs but to do and die," wrote Alfred, Lord Tennyson in "The Charge of the Light Brigade."

Modern warfare has changed that way of thinking. Soldiers no longer form themselves into long lines and shoot at each other. They maneuver in small units in which every man is prepared to assume the leader's role. Conditions on a battlefield change constantly. Specific orders given a few hours before may no longer make sense. Soldiers are trained to focus on their main goal while adapting or changing their original orders when conditions require. In other words, a soldier is expected to think.

• BAR MITZVAH •

The same could be said of *mitzvot,* the commandments God gave the Jewish people. Some say *mitzvot* are to be followed without question; that they are just as valid today as they were for ages past. Others would say that the twentieth and the twenty-first centuries are vastly different from any other time. The Commanding General's original orders may no longer apply, and He hasn't issued new ones. So what is a loyal soldier to do?

A loyal soldier focuses on his mission's main goal. As he moves forward, he tries to follow his commander's orders as much as possible, but he is also prepared to think for himself.

So it is with becoming bar mitzvah. As a boy takes on *mitzvot,* the responsibilities of Jewish manhood, he must keep the main goals of Judaism in mind by asking himself these questions:

- What does God want and expect of me?
- Will my actions strengthen my ties with the Jewish people in every time and place?
- Will my actions help my family, my neighbors, my fellow citizens, my fellow human beings, and the creatures who share the world with me?

We must strive to make the world a better place. In the words of *Miss Rumphius,* a wise and lovely picture book by the artist and writer Barbara Cooney, we must ask ourselves, "What can I do to make the world more beautiful?"

A story is told about Rabbi Ya'akov Yitzhak, known to his followers as The Yehudi (The Jew) of Przysucha. He was once asked, "The Talmud says the stork is called *hasidah,* the loving one, because she shows such devotion to her mate and her nestlings."

"That is true," the Yehudi answered.

"Then why is she classified among the unclean birds?"

The Yehudi thought a minute. Then he said, "Because she gives her love only to her own."

Bar mitzvah is not just about becoming a man.

It is not even about becoming a Jew.

It is about becoming a human being.

INTERVIEW ·····················

I can't say that my bar mitzvah made any great changes in my life. More important than the ceremony itself was the studying I did before and after I became bar mitzvah. It was all natural.

I had a place for myself in the shul, *the synagogue. It had a charged atmosphere every Shabbos, every Sabbath. I was a mascot of the old men. I loved to plug in with the last generation. I had a battle with my mother when she wanted me to start wearing* tzitzit *and putting on tefillin. I won.*

On the night before my bar mitzvah, I was so nervous that the cantor had to give me a glass of schnapps to keep me going. On the day of my bar mitzvah, Mr. Rosenbaum sang with me to keep me on tune. I was exhausted when it was over. My parents had no money, but I was adamant about having a party. So we had a little lunch in the shul. *I remember I had a new suit.*

What did I get for bar mitzvah gifts? I remember I got one fountain pen, a baseball mitt that I used once, and two books on archaeology. Very important books, too, considering my later career. I grew up to become a Bible scholar. After I learned Hebrew, I studied Arabic and other languages of the Middle East.

It was a good bar mitzvah. I got even more out of it than I expected. I was happy. It was exactly the bar mitzvah I wanted.

Yochanan Muffs
Bar Mitzvah, 1945

INTERVIEW ·····································

I certainly can't say that my bar mitzvah was a spiritual experience, but it did something very important. It planted a seed.

I became bar mitzvah in the sixties. My friends and I were the first baby boomers. Our fathers came back from World War II, married, and started raising families. There were lots of kids running around our suburban neighborhood, so hardly a week went by in our synagogue without at least one bar mitzvah celebration.

Bar mitzvah meant one thing: the party. The party was a major social event for our parents. They didn't care much about the religious aspect. However, you couldn't have the party without the ceremony. So for years, my friends and I had to spend two or three days a week in Hebrew school, plus going to services on Saturday. Add the year you spend studying your haftarah, and it comes to a huge investment of time. We resented it. It wasn't pleasant for our teachers either. Most were Europeans who didn't understand or especially like American kids.

The challenge was getting a boy to do something he didn't want to do, so the parents could have a big party that the boy really didn't care about. So naturally the parents used pressure and bribery.

What can I say about my bar mitzvah? It was vulgar, crass, thoroughly unspiritual, and my parents spent far too much money for all the wrong reasons. And yet . . . something happened in spite of that. Through the long process of preparing for my bar mitzvah, I learned I was Jewish and received the barest taste of what that might mean. Years later, I would come to know more, much more.

Now, as a parent, I can appreciate what my parents accomplished. Despite my misgivings at the time and my disagreement with their priorities, they succeeded in preserving my Jewishness.

I don't believe that could ever have happened without that first small taste, that tiny little seed.

Howard Berkowitz
Bar Mitzvah, 1961

GLOSSARY

Aliyah (ah-lee-YAH or ah-LEE-yah) is the honor of being called up to the Torah to say the blessings that precede and follow the reading of each selection. Plural: *aliyot* (ah-lee-YOAT)

Aron Kodesh (ah-RON KO-desh) is the cabinet or ark where the Torah scrolls are stored. The *aron kodesh* is usually placed on the side of the synagogue facing Jerusalem.

Ashkenazic (ash-ken-AZ-ic) refers to Jews living in the Christian countries of Europe. *Ashkenaz* is an unknown land originally mentioned in the Bible. It is the old Hebrew name for Germany.

B.C.E. stands for Before the Common Era. (**C.E.** stands for Common Era.) Jewish people prefer to use these initials instead of the Christian-oriented terms B.C. (Before Christ) and A.D. (*Anno Domini,* "in the Year of Our Lord").

Baal korei (bahl KO-RAY or bahl KO-ray) is the person who reads from the Torah scroll during the synagogue service.

Bar Mitzvah (bar mitz-VAH or bar MITZ-vah) is a boy who has reached the age of thirteen years and one day. He is now considered ready to take on the responsibilities of a Jewish adult. The words mean "One who has the obligation of fulfilling commandments." Plural: *bnai mitzvah.*

Bat Mitzvah (baht mitz-VAH or baht MITZ-vah) is a girl who has reached the age of twelve years and one day. She is now considered ready to take on the responsibilities of a Jewish adult. The words also mean "One who has the obligation of fulfilling commandments." The bat mitzvah ceremony became a Jewish tradition during the twentieth century. Plural: *bnot mitzvah.*

Bimah (bee-MAH or BEE-mah) is the raised platform, usually located on the synagogue's eastern side, with a large desk on which the Torah scroll is read. The word means "elevated place."

Dvar Torah (duh-VAR toe-RAH or duh-VAR TOE-ruh) is a sermon based on the weekly Torah reading.

Golel (go-LAYL or GO-layl) is the person given the honor of rolling up the Torah scroll at the conclusion of the weekly reading.

Haftarah (hahf-tah-RAH or hahf-TOE-rah) is a reading from the Prophets that supplements the weekly Torah portion. Plural: *haftarot* (haf-tar-OAT)

Hasidim (ha-see-DEEM or ha-SEED-eem) are members of special communities within Orthodox Judaism who believe that their rabbis, or *rebbes*, have a unique relationship with God. Hasidim have rich musical and story traditions. They worship with great enthusiasm and joy.

Kippah (kee-PAH) is a skullcap, the head covering traditionally worn by men and boys during the synagogue service. Plural: *kippot* (kee-POAT)

Kohen (ko-HAYN or KO-hayn) is a priest or a descendant of priests. The priests conducted the sacrificial services until the destruction of the Second Temple in 70 C.E. Plural: *kohanim* (ko-han-EEM)

Kosher (Kah-SHER or KO-sher) describes food that meets the requirements of the Jewish dietary laws and is permissible for Jews to eat.

• Glossary •

Kotel (KO-TELL or KO-tell) is an abbreviation of *Kotel Ha'maar-avi,* the Western Wall in Israel. The *Kotel* is one of the last vestiges of the Second Temple.

Levi (Lay-VEE or LAY-vee) is a Levite or a descendant of Levites. The Levites assisted the priests in the sacrificial service. Plural: *leviim* (le-vee-EEM or le-VEE-im)

Maftir (mahf-TEER or MAHF-teer) is the person who reads the haftarah.

Magbehah (mag-BEE-ah) is the person given the honor of lifting and holding up the Torah scroll at the conclusion of the Torah reading.

Minyan (min-YAHN or MIN-yahn) is the quorum of ten Jews needed to hold a prayer service. Orthodox synagogues count only men; liberal synagogues include women.

Mishkan (mish-KAHN) is the tent sanctuary or tabernacle where the Israelites worshiped during the time of Moses.

Mitzvah (mitz-VAH or MITZ-vah) is a religious commandment. According to tradition, Jews are responsible for fulfilling 613 positive and negative commandments. Plural: *mitzvot* (mitz-VOAT)

Musaf (mu-SAHF or MU-sahf) is the additional group of prayers that concludes the Sabbath morning synagogue service.

137

Ner Tamid (ner tah-MEED or ner TOH-mid) is the "eternal light" that hangs before the *aron kodesh*.

Parashah (pa-ra-SHAH or PAR-shuh) is the weekly selection from the Torah chanted during the Sabbath service. Plural: *parshiyot* (par-shee-YOAT)

Rabbi (RAB-eye) is a Jewish religious leader. The word means "master" or "teacher." Plural: rabbis or *rabbanim* (rahb-bahn-EEM)

Sephardic (Se-PHAR-dic) refers to Jews with roots in the Muslim countries of Spain, North Africa, the Middle East, and Central Asia. *Sepharad* is the old Hebrew term for Spain. The ancestors of many Sephardic Jews, who originally lived in Spain, were driven out by Ferdinand and Isabella in 1492.

Shema (shuh-MA) is one of the most important Jewish prayers. It begins with the words, "Hear, O Israel, The Lord, our God, The Lord is One."

Tallit (tal-LEET) or *tallis* (TALL-us) is a prayer shawl worn during morning services. Plural: *tallitot* (tal-leet-OAT) or *tallesim* (tah-LACE-im)

Talmud (tahl-MOOD or TAHL-mood) is the authoritative compendium of Jewish traditions, parables, custom, and law, as well as related commentaries. The Talmud was compiled between the second and sixth centuries C.E.

Tefillin (Tuh-feel-EEN or tuh-FILL-in) are leather boxes containing verses from the Torah which traditional Jews wear on their heads and left arms during morning prayers. Tefillin are not worn on festivals or Sabbaths.

Torah (Toe-RAH or TOE-ruh) can refer to either (1) the Pentateuch, also called the Five Books of Moses (Genesis, Exodus, Leviticus, Numbers, and Deuteronomy); (2) the entire body of Jewish law and its commentaries; or (3) the parchment scroll on which the Five Books of Moses are written.

Tzitzit (tzee-TZEET) or *tzitzis* (TZITZ-iss) is a special fringe or tassel attached to each of the four corners of a tallit. Plural: *tzitziyot* (tzee-tzee-YOAT).

Yad (yahd) is a pointer, usually made of silver. The *baal korei* uses a *yad* when reading from the Torah Scroll to avoid touching the parchment. The Hebrew word means "hand."

INDEX